# SUBJECT GUIDE TO CLASSICAL INSTRUMENTAL MUSIC

by
Jennifer Goodenberger

The Scarecrow Press, Inc.
Metuchen, N.J. & London
1989

British Library Cataloguing-in-Publication data available

Library of Congress Cataloging-in-Publication Data

Goodenberger, Jennifer, 1957-
    Subject guide to classical instrumental music / by Jennifer
Goodenberger.
        p.    cm.
    Bibliography: p.
    Includes index.
    ISBN 0-8108-2209-1
    1. Instrumental music--Bibliography.   2. Program music--
Bibliography.   I. Title.
ML128.I65G59    1989                              89-4129
016.781'56--dc19

*The painter turns a poem into a painting;
the musician sets a picture to music.*

*Robert Schumann*

# CONTENTS

# FOREWORD

For centuries composers have found inspiration for their compositions in extra–musical sources and in the world around them. Beethoven conceived ideas from nature for his Sixth Symphony, the *Pastoral.* Messiaen incorporated bird calls into his *Oiseaux Exotiques* (Exotic birds). The visual arts and literature have evoked the imagination, as in Mussorgsky's *Pictures at an Exhibition* and Strauss's *Don Quixote.* The term used to describe this music is program, or programmatic, music which draws from outside itself for inspiration. Most compositions in this guide are classified by their programmatic content.

In addition to program works, those which have been nicknamed by the composer, the publisher or the public are also included. These compositions were not composed with a program in mind, but bring an idea to the listener. An example is Beethoven's Piano Sonata No. 14, the *Moonlight.*

This book concerns the instrumental repertoire. It is not an exhaustive study, but a general guide. Compositions were chosen for their accessibility in libraries, record stores, concert halls, and music reference books. Occasionally, opera has been included when it has a central theme which can be categorized. Verdi's *Macbeth,* listed under SHAKESPEARE, and Wagner's *Tristan und Isolde,* under LOVERS, are examples of operas which have a main theme. Within an opera are instrumental works such as overtures, interludes, preludes to acts, and dances. These often draw musically from the vocal themes and can be programmatically derived.

The earliest works date from the 1600's. The latest are by contemporary composers. The majority of compositions are from the 19th century. This was a time when composers drew heavily upon outside sources to stimulate their imagination and evoke, compositionally, the metaphors of that era.

There are 208 categories in this book. The larger have been subdivided: BIRDS, CITIES, GREEK MYTHS, LITERATURE (by author), and SHAKESPEARE (by play). Each entry includes composer, title, translation, nickname, opus number, and type of work, (e.g., Orchestral work, Piano). A work is categorized by its overall program. Should the composition have multiple movements, they are listed and placed in their own categories. Works in italics are titles; works in quotes are movements.

The audience for this book includes individuals working in film, television, radio, and education. Producers of films and television programs may find it helpful in selecting easily accessible music which can tie into visual themes. Radio programmers can select various motifs to serve as themes for shows. Teachers can use this guide to select specific musical themes for study and to enhance interdisciplinary instruction.

In the process of compiling and writing this book I had the help and support of many friends and colleagues. In particular I would like to thank KMUN–FM in Astoria, Oregon. My work there as a classical music

programmer taught me the need for a book such as this. The Clatsop
Community College Library and the Astor Public Library have both been
wonderful in supplying books to study, and allowing me to keep them far
beyond their due date. Image Designworks prepared the manuscript, and
has done an excellent job with design and typesetting. Many friends lent me
support, but in particular I would like to thank Barbara Freeman and David
Weers who gave great and continued counsel. My family has been
unwavering in their support and help, especially my parents, John and
Peggy. They have guided me and listened to my fears and joys. My father
has also helped with the technical and printing aspects. My deep
appreciation to all.


Jennifer Goodenberger
Astoria, Oregon
January, 1989

# SUBJECT GUIDE

# A

AFFECTIONS — see also Joy, Tragic

Beethoven, Ludwig van (1770–1827)
  Sonata No. 8 in C minor *Pathétique*. Opus 13. Piano.
  Sonata No. 17 in D minor *Tempest*. Opus 31, No. 2. Piano.
  Sonata No. 23 in F minor *Appassionata*. Opus 57. Piano.
  Quartet No. 11 in F minor *Serious*. Opus 95. String quartet.
Bloch, Ernest (1880–1959)
  "1861 – 1865. Hours of Joy – Hours of Sorrow" from *America: An Epic Rhapsody*. Orchestral work.
Falla, Manuel de (1876–1946)
  "Scene of Sorrowing Love" and "Dance of Terror" from *El Amor brujo* (Love, the magician). Ballet.
Hanson, Howard (1896–1981)
  *Four Poems*. Opus 9. Piano. (1) "Peace" (2) "Joy" (3) "Yearning" (4) "Desire."
Haydn, Franz Joseph (1732–1809)
  Symphony No. 26 in D minor *Lamentatione* (Lamentation).
  Symphony No. 44 in E minor *Trauer* (Sad).
  Symphony No. 49 in F minor *La Passione* (The passion).
Hindemith, Paul (1895–1963)
  *The Four Temperaments*. Violin, viola, cello and piano. (1) "Melancholic" (2) "Sanguine" (3) "Phlegmatic" (4) "Choleric."
Messiaen, Olivier (1908–
  "Amen of the Agony of Jesus" and "Amen of Desire" from *Visions de l' amen*. Two pianos.
Nielsen, Carl (1865–1931)
  Symphony No. 2 *The Four Temperaments*. Opus 16.
Scriabin, Alexander (1872–1915)
  Sonata No. 4 in F–sharp major *Desire and Anguish*. Opus 30. Piano.
Tchaikovsky, Peter Ilyich (1840–1893)
  Symphony No. 6 in B minor *Pathétique*. Opus 74.
Wolf, Hugo (1860–1903)
  "Combats, Passions, Frenzy, Annihilation" from *Penthesilea*. Orchestral work.

AFRICA — see also Blacks

Godowsky, Leopold (1870–1938)
"Ethiopian Serenade" from *Triakontameron*. Piano.
"Nocturnal Tangier" from *Triakontameron*. Piano.
Meyerbeer, Giacomo (1791–1864)
*L'Africaine* (The African woman). Opera.
Milhaud, Darius (1892–1974)
*La Création du monde* (The creation of the world). Opus 81a. Ballet.
Poulenc, Francis (1899–1963)
*Rapsodie nègre*. Chamber orchestra.
Rossini, Gioacchino (1792–1868)
*L'Italiana in Algeri* (The Italian girl in Algiers). Opera.
Saint-Saëns, Camille (1835–1921)
*Africa*. Opus 89. Piano and orchestra.
*Suite algerienne* (Algerian suite). Opus 60. Orchestral work.
Still, William Grant (1895–1978)
*Africa*. Orchestral work.


AFTERNOON — see also Day, Evening, Morning, Night, Noon,
Sunrise, Sunset

Debussy, Claude (1862–1918)
*Prélude à l'après–midi d'un faune* (Prelude to the afternoon of a faun).
Orchestral work.
Haydn, Franz Joseph (1732–1809)
Symphony No. 7 in C major *Le Midi* (Afternoon).
Siegmeister, Elie (1909–
"Lazy Afternoon" from *Ozark Set*. Orchestral work.


ANGELS — see also Heaven, Spirits

Gluck, Christoph Willibald (1714–1787)
"Dance of the Blessed Spirits" from *Orpheus and Eurydice*.
Orchestral work.
Hindemith, Paul (1895–1963)
"The Concert of the Angel" from *Mathis der Maler* (Matthias the
painter). Opera; orchestral work.
Messiaen, Olivier (1908–
"Amen of the Angels, of the Saints, of the Song of the Birds" from
*Visions de l'amen*. Two pianos.

"Vocalise, pour l'ange qui annonce la fin du temps" (Vocalise, for the angel who announces the end of time) and "Fouillis d'arcs–en–ciel, pour l'ange qui annonce la fin du temps" (Cluster of rainbows, for the angel who announces the end of time) from *Quatuor pour la fin du temps* (Quartet for the end of time). Clarinet, violin, cello, piano.

Respighi, Ottorino (1879–1936)
"San Michele arcangelo" (The archangel Michael) from *Vetrate di chiesa* (Church windows). Orchestral work.

Ruggles, Carl (1876–1971)
*Angels*. Four violins, 3 cellos.

Subotnick, Morton (1933–
"Angels (A Fluttering of Wings)" from *The Double Life of Amphibians*. String quartet.

ANIMALS — see also Bears, Birds, Butterflies, Cats, Elephants, Fish, Horses, Insects

Bartók, Béla (1881–1945)
"Song of the Fox" from *Mikrokosmos*. Book 3. Piano.

Copland, Aaron (1900–
*The Cat and the Mouse*. Piano.

Haydn, Franz Joseph (1732–1809)
Quartet No. 49 in D major *Froschquartett* (Frog quartet). Opus 50, No. 6. String quartet.

Hovhaness, Alan (1911–
*And God Created Whales*. Orchestral work.

Poulenc, Francis (1899–1963)
*Les Animaux modèles* (Model animals). Ballet.

Prokofiev, Sergei (1891–1953)
*Peter and the Wolf*. Opus 67. Narrator and orchestra.

Respighi, Ottorino (1879–1936)
"Butantan" (In a snake garden near Sao Paulo) from *Impressioni brasiliane* (Brazilian impressions). Orchestral work.

Rieti, Vittorio (1898–
"March of the Animals" from *L'Arca di Noé* (Noah's Ark). Orchestral work.

Saint–Saëns, Camille (1835–1921)
*Le Carnaval des animaux: fantaisie zoologique* (Carnival of the animals: grand zoological fantasy). Orchestral work. Fourteen movements: (1) "Introduction and Royal Lions' March" (2) "Hens and Cocks" (3) "Hemiones – Swift Animals" (4) "Tortoises" (5) "The Elephant" (6) "Kangaroos" (7) "Aquarium" (8) "Long–eared Personages" (9) "The Cuckoo in the Depths of the Wood" (10) "The Aviary" (11) "Pianists" (12) "Fossils" (13) "The Swan" (14) "Finale."

Thomson, Virgil (1896–
"Cattle" from *The Plow that Broke the Plains*. Orchestral work.
Villa–Lobos, Heitor (1887–1959)
*Os animalinhos* (Little toy animals) from *Prole do bêbê* (Baby's playthings). No. 2. Piano. Eight movements: (1) "Cardboard Cat" (2) "Toy Mouse" (3) "Rubber Dog" (4) "Wooden Horse" (5) "Tin Ox" (6) "Cloth Bird" (7) "Cotton Bear" (8) "Glass Wolf."


## ARABIA

Grieg, Edvard (1843–1907)
"Arab Dance" from *Peer Gynt*. Suite No. 2. Opus 55. Orchestral work.
Rabaud, Henri (1873–1949)
*Mârouf*. Opera. (Inspired by *The Arabian Nights*.)
Rimsky–Korsakov, Nikolai (1844–1908)
*Scheherazade*. Opus 35. Orchestral work. Four movements: (1) "The Sea and Sinbad's Ship" (2) "The Kalendar Prince" (3) "The Young Prince" (4) "Festival at Baghdad – The Sea – The Ship Founders on The Rock."
Symphony No. 2 *Antar*. Opus 9.
Schuller, Gunther (1925–
"Arabian Town" from *Seven Studies on Themes of Paul Klee*. Orchestral work.
Strauss, Johann Jr. (1825–1899)
*Tausend und eine Nacht* (A thousand and one nights). Opus 346. Waltz.
Tchaikovsky, Peter Ilyich (1840–1893)
"Arabian Dance" from *The Nutcracker*. Opus 71. Ballet.
Weber, Carl Maria von (1786–1826)
*Abu Hassan*. Opera.


## ARMENIA

Hovhaness, Alan (1911–
*Armenian Rhapsody No. 1*. Opus 45.
*Armenian Rhapsody No. 3*. Opus 189.
*Khaldis*. Opus 91. Piano and orchestra.
*Six Dances for Piano:* (1) "Yerangi" (2) "Ounapi" (3) "Marali" (4) "Shoushigi" (5) "Hed–arach" (6) "Choror."

# ART

Berlioz, Hector (1803–1869)
  *Benvenuto Cellini.* Opus 23. Opera.
  *Le Carnaval romain* (Roman carnival). Opus 9. Orchestral work.
    (Inspired by Benvenuto Cellini.)
Collins, Anthony (1893–1963)
  *Hogarth Suite.* Oboe and strings. (Inspired by William Hogarth.)
Debussy, Claude (1862–1918)
  *Estampes* (Engravings). Piano. Three movements: (1) "Pagodes"
    (2) "Soirée dans Grenade" (Evening party in Grenada) (3) "Jardins
    sous la pluie" (Gardens in the rain). (Inspired by Japanese prints.)
  *L'Isle joyeuse* (The island of joy). Piano. (Inspired by Jean Antoine
    Watteau.)
Dopper, Cornelis (1870–1939)
  Symphony No. 2 *Rembrandt.*
Gade, Niels (1817–1890)
  *Michelangelo.* Opus 39. Orchestral work.
Godowsky, Leopold (1870–1938)
  *Watteau Landscape.* Two pianos.
Granados, Enrique (1867–1916)
  *Goyescas.* Piano. Six movements: (1) "Los requiebros" (Gallant
    compliments) (2) "Coloquio en la reja" (Conversation through the
    grilled window) (3) "El Fandango del candil" (Fandango by
    candlelight) (4) "Quejas o la maja y el ruiseñor" (The maid and the
    nightingale) (5) "El Amor y la muerte" (Love and death)
    (6) "Epílogo: la serenade del espectro" (Serenade of the specter).
    (Inspired by Goya.)
Hindemith, Paul (1895–1963)
  *Mathis der Maler* (Matthias the painter). Opera; orchestral work.
    Three movements: (1) "The Concert of the Angels"
    (2) "The Entombment" (3) "Temptation of St. Anthony."
Hovhaness, Alan (1911–
  *Fantasy on Japanese Woodprints.* Opus 211. Xylophone and
    orchestra.
  *Fra Angelico.* Opus 220. Orchestral work.
Huber, Hans (1852–1921)
  Symphony No. 2. Opus 115. (Inspired by Arnold Böcklin.)
  Symphony No. 3. Opus 118. (Inspired by Hans Holbein.)
Liszt, Franz (1811–1886)
  "Il Pensieroso" (The thoughtful one) from *Années de pèlerinage:
    Seconde année: Italie* (Years of pilgrimage: second year: Italy).
    Piano. (Inspired by Michelangelo.)
  "Sposalizio" (Wedding) from *Années de pèlerinage: Seconde année:
    Italie* (Years of pilgrimage: second year: Italy). Piano.
    (Inspired by Raphael.)
  *Totentanz* (*Danse macabre* ) (Dance of death). Piano and orchestra.
    (Inspired by Ocragna.)

Martinu, Bohuslav (1890–1959)
"The Parable of Sculpture" from *Parables*. Orchestral work.
Mussorgsky, Modest (1839–1881)
*Pictures at an Exhibition*. Piano; orchestral work. Eleven movements:
(1) "Promenade" (2) "Gnomes" (3) "The Old Castle"
(4) "Tuileries" (5) "Bydlo" (6) "Ballet of the Chicks in their Shells"
(7) "Samuel Goldenberg and Schmuyle" (8) "The Market Place at
Limoges" (9) "Catacombs" (10) "A Hut on Fowl's Legs" (Baba
Yaga) (11) "The Great Gate at Kiev." (Inspired by Victor
Hartmann.)
Rachmaninoff, Sergei (1873–1943)
*Toteninsel* (The isle of the dead). Opus 29. Orchestral work.
(Inspired by Arnold Böcklin.)
Reger, Max (1873–1916)
*Vier Tondichtungen nach Arnold Böcklin*. (Four tone poems after
Böcklin). Opus 128. Orchestral work. (1) "Der geigende Eremit"
(The hermit with the violin) (2) "Im Spiel der Wellen" (Among the
play of the waves) (3) "Die Toteninsel" (Isle of the dead)
(4) "Bacchanale."
Respighi, Ottorino (1879–1936)
*Trittico botticelliano* (Botticellian triptych). Three movements:
(1) "Primavera" (Spring) (2) "L'Adorazione dei Magi" (The
adoration of the Magi) (3) "La Nascita di Venere" (The birth of
Venus). (Inspired by Sandro Botticelli.) Orchestral work.
Rózycki, Ludomir (1884–1953)
*Mona Lisa Gioconda*. Opus 29. Orchestral work.
(Inspired by Leonardo da Vinci.)
Schuller, Gunther (1925–
*American Triptych: Studies in Texture*. Orchestral work. (1) "Four
Directions" (Alexander Calder) (2) "Out of the Web" (Jackson
Pollock) (3) "Swing Landscape" (Stuart Davis).
*Seven Studies on Themes of Paul Klee*. Orchestral work.
(1) "Antique Harmonies" (2) "Abstract Trio" (3) "Little Blue Devil"
(4) "The Twittering Machine" (5) "Arabian Town" (6) "An Eerie
Moment" (7) "Pastorale."
Strauss, Johann Jr. (1825–1899)
*Künstlerleben* (Artist's life). Opus 316. Waltz.
Strong, George Templeton (1856–1948)
*Sintram*. Symphony. (Inspired by Albrecht Dürer.)
Thomson, Virgil (1896–
"Bugles and Birds (A Portait of Pablo Picasso)" from *Portraits*.
Album 1. Piano.
Walton, William (1902–1983)
*Portsmouth Point*. Orchestral work. (Inspired by Thomas
Rowlandson.)
*Scapino*. Orchestral work. (Inspired by Jacques Callot.)
White, Felix (1884–1945)
*Astarte syriaca*. Orchestral work. (Inspired by Dante Gabriel
Rossetti.)

AUTUMN — see also Seasons, Spring, Summer, Winter

Bax, Arnold (1883–1953)
*November Woods.* Orchestral work.
Delius, Frederick (1862–1934)
"Autumn" from *North Country Sketches.* Orchestral work.
Glazunov, Alexander (1865–1936)
*The Seasons.* Opus 67. Ballet.
Grieg, Edvard (1843–1907)
*In Autumn.* Opus 11. Orchestral work.
Hadley, Henry (1871–1937)
"Autumn" from Symphony No. 2 *The Four Seasons.* Opus 30.
MacDowell, Edward (1860–1908)
"In Autumn" from *Woodland Sketches.* Opus 51. Piano.
"In October" from *Suite No. 1.* Opus 42. Orchestral work.
"The Joy of Autumn" from *New England Idyls.* Opus 62. Piano.
Moore, Douglas (1893–1969)
*A Symphony of Autumn.*
Prokofiev, Sergei (1891–1953)
*Esquisses automnales* (Autumn sketches). Opus 8. Orchestral work.
Tchaikovsky, Peter Ilyich (1840–1893)
"October: Autumn Song" from *The Seasons.* Opus 37b. Piano.
Thomson, Virgil (1896–
*Autumn.* Harpsichord, strings and percussion.
Vivaldi, Antonio (1678–1741)
Concerto in F, "L'Autunno," from *Le quattro stagioni* (The four seasons). Opus 8, No. 3. Violin and orchestra.

# B

BEARS — see also Animals

Bartók, Béla (1881–1945)
"Bear Dance" from *Ten Easy Pieces.* Piano.
Elgar, Edward (1857–1934)
"The Tame Bear" and "Wild Bears" from *Wand of Youth Suite* No. 2.
Opus 1b. Orchestral work.
Haydn, Franz Joseph (1732–1809)
Symphony No. 82 in C major *L'Ours* (The bear).
MacDowell, Edward (1860–1908)
"Visit of the Bear" from *Moon Pictures.* Piano duet.
Villa–Lobos, Heitor (1887–1959)
"Cotton Bear" from *Os animalinhos* (Little toy animals) from
*Prole do bêbê* (Baby's playthings) No. 2. Piano.

Walton, William (1902–1983)
*The Bear.* Opera.


BELLS — see also Clock

Debussy, Claude (1862–1918)
"Cloches à travers les feuilles" (Bells through the leaves)
from *Images II.* Piano.
Dvořák, Antonín (1841–1904)
Symphony No. 1 in C minor *The Bells of Zlonice.* Opus 3.
Elgar, Edward (1857–1934)
"The Little Bells" from *Wand of Youth Suite* No. 2. Opus 1b.
Orchestral work.
Falla, Manuel de (1876–1946)
"Morning Chimes" from *El Amor brujo* (Love, the magician).
Ballet.
Ketelbey, Albert (1875–1959)
*Bells Across the Meadows.* Orchestral work.
Liszt, Franz (1811–1886)
"La Campanella" (Little bell) from *Etudes d' exécution transcendante
d' après Paganini* (Transcendental Etudes after Paganini). Piano.
"Les Cloches de Genève" (The bells of Geneva) from *Années de
pèlerinage: Première année: Suisse* (Years of pilgrimage: first
year: Switzerland). Piano.
Paganini, Niccolò (1782–1840)
"Rondo à la clochette" (Bell rondo) from Concerto No. 2 in B minor.
Opus 7. Violin and orchestra.
Ravel, Maurice (1875–1937)
"La Vallée des cloches" (The valley of bells) from *Miroirs* (Mirrors).
Piano.
Toch, Ernst (1887–1964)
*Big Ben.* Opus 62. Orchestral work.


The BIBLE — see also Christ, Christmas, Easter, Jewish

Alfvén, Hugo (1872–1960)
*The Prodigal Son.* Orchestral work.
Bernstein, Leonard (1918–
Symphony *Jeremiah.* Mezzo–soprano and orchestra.
Bloch, Ernest (1880–1959)
*Schelomo* (Solomon). Cello and orchestra.
Castelnuovo–Tedesco, Mario (1895–1968)
Concerto No. 2 *The Prophets.* Violin and orchestra.
Three movements: (1) "Isaiah" (2) "Jeremiah" (3) "Elijah."

*Naomi and Ruth.* Ballet.
*Noah's Ark.* Orchestral work.
Creston, Paul (1906–1985)
 *Corinthians: XIII.* Opus 82. Orchestral work.
Dello Joio, Norman (1913–
 *Meditations on Ecclesiastes.* String orchestra.
Haydn, Franz Joseph (1732–1809)
 *Die Sieben Worte des Erlösers am Kreuze.* (The seven last words of
 the savior on the cross). Orchestral work.
Honegger, Arthur (1892–1955)
 *Le Roi David* (King David). Opera.
Jacobi, Frederick (1891–1952)
 *Hagiographia.* Three Biblical narratives. String quartet and piano.
Kuhnau, Johann (1660–1722)
 *Biblical Sonatas.* Harpsichord. Six sonatas: (1) "The Fight between
 David and Goliath" (2) "Saul cured by David through Music"
 (3) "Jacob's Wedding" (4) "Hezekiah, Sick unto Death and
 Restored to Health" (5) "Gideon, Savior of Israel" (6) "Jacob's
 Death and Burial."
 "The Fight between David and Goliath" from *Biblical Sonatas.*
 Harpsichord. Six movements: (1) "The Bravado of Goliath"
 (2) "The Terror of the Israelites and Their Prayer to God"
 (3) "David's Courage Before the Terrible Enemy" (4) "The Dispute
 and the Slinging of the Stone by David" (5) "The Plight of the
 Philistines" (6) "Paeans of Victory by the Israelites."
Messiaen, Olivier (1908–
 *Colours of The Celestial City.* Orchestral work. (Inspired by
 *Revelations.*)
 *Et Exspecto resurrectionem mortuorum* (And I await the resurrection
 of the dead). Orchestral work.
Milhaud, Darius (1892–1974)
 *David.* Opera.
Rieti, Vittorio (1898–
 *L'Arca di Noé* (Noah's Ark). Orchestral work. Five movements:
 (1) "Prelude to the First Tableau" (2) "The Flood" (3) "Prelude to
 the Second Tableau" (4) "March of the Animals"
 (5) "The Rainbow."
Saint–Saëns, Camille (1835–1921)
 *Samson et Dalila.* Opus 47. Opera.
Saminsky, Lazare (1882–1959)
 *Jephtha's Daughter.* Opera, ballet.
Schmitt, Florent (1870–1958)
 *La Tragedie de Salomé.* Opus 50. Ballet.
Schönberg, Arnold (1874–1951)
 *Moses und Aron.* Opera.
Schuman, William (1910–
 *Judith.* Concerto for dancer and orchestra.
Strauss, Richard (1864–1949)
 *Salome.* Opera.

Vaughan Williams, Ralph (1872–1958)
*Job–A Masque for Dancing.* Ballet.
Zádor, Eugene (1894–1977)
*Biblical Scenes.* Orchestral work. Three movements: (1) "Joseph"
(2) "David" (3) "Paul."


BIRDS — see also Animals

CHICKENS and ROOSTERS

Haydn, Franz Joseph (1732–1809)
Symphony No. 83 in G minor *Poule* (The hen).
Mason, Daniel Gregory (1873–1953)
*Chanticleer.* Orchestral work. (Inspired by Thoreau.)
Mussorgsky, Modest (1839–1881)
"Ballet of Chicks in Their Shells" from *Pictures at an Exhibition.*
Piano; orchestral work.
Respighi, Ottorino (1879–1936)
"La Gallina" (The hen) from *Gli Uccelli* (The birds). Orchestral
work.
Rimsky–Korsakov, Nikolai (1844–1908)
*Le Coq d'or* (The golden cockerel). Opera.
Saint–Saëns, Camille (1835–1921)
"Hens and Cocks" from *Le Carnaval des animaux: fantaisie
zoologique* (Carnival of the animals). Orchestral work.

CUCKOOS

Daquin, Louis (1694–1772)
*Le Coucou* (The cuckoo). Harpsichord.
Delius, Frederick (1862–1934)
*On Hearing the First Cuckoo in Spring.* Orchestral work.
Frescobaldi, Girolamo (1583–1643)
*Capriccio on The Cuckoo's Call.* Harpsichord.
Handel, George Frideric (1685–1759)
Concerto No. 13 in F major *The Cuckoo and the Nightingale.*
Organ and orchestra.
Respighi, Ottorino (1879–1936)
"Il Cucu" (The cuckoo) from *Gli Uccelli* (The birds). Orchestral
work.
Saint–Saëns, Camille (1835–1921)
"The Cuckoo in the Depths of the Wood" from *Le Carnaval des
animaux: fantaisie zoologique* (Carnival of the animals).
Orchestral work.

## DOVES

Dvořák, Antonín (1841–1904)
*The Wild Dove.* Opus 110. Orchestral work.
Respighi, Ottorino (1879–1936)
"La Colomba" (The dove) from *Gli Uccelli* (The birds). Orchestral
work.

## LARKS

Haydn, Franz Joseph (1732–1809)
Quartet No. 67 in D major *Lerchenquartett* (Lark quartet). Opus
64, No. 5. String quartet.
Tchaikovsky, Peter Ilyich (1840–1893)
"March: Song of the Lark" from *The Seasons.* Opus 37b. Piano.
Vaughan Williams, Ralph (1872–1958)
*The Lark Ascending.* Violin and orchestra.

## NIGHTINGALES

Couperin, François (1631–1701)
"Le Rossignol–en–amour" (The nightingale in love). Ordre 14,
No. 1. Harpsichord.
"Le Rossignol–vainqueur" (The triumphant nightingale). Ordre 14,
No. 4. Harpsichord.
Granados, Enrique (1867–1916)
"Quejas o la maja y el ruiseñor" (The maid and the nightingale)
from *Goyescas.* Piano.
Handel, George Frideric (1685–1759)
Concerto No. 13 in F major *The Cuckoo and the Nightingale.*
Organ and orchestra.
Respighi, Ottorino (1879–1936)
"L'Usignuolo" (The nightingale) from *Gli Uccelli* (The birds).
Orchestral work.
Stravinsky, Igor (1882–1971)
*Le Chant du rossignol* (The song of the nightingale). Ballet;
orchestral work. Three movements: (1) "The Palace of the
Chinese Emperor" (2) "The Two Nightingales" (3) "Illness
and Recovery of the Chinese Emperor."
*Le Rossignol* (The nightingale). Opera.

## PEACOCKS

Griffes, Charles Tomlinson (1884–1920)
"The White Peacock" from *Four Roman Sketches.* Opus 7, No. 1.
Piano; orchestral work.

Kodály, Zoltán (1882–1967)
*Variations on a Hungarian Folksong* (Peacock variations).
Orchestral work.

## SWANS

Gottschalk, Louis Moreau (1829–1869)
*The Dying Swan.* Opus 100. Piano.
MacDowell, Edward (1860–1908)
"The Swan" from *Moon Pictures.* Opus 21. Piano duet.
Saint–Saëns, Camille (1835–1921)
"Le Cygne" (The swan) from *Le Carnaval des animaux: fantaisie
zoologique* (Carnival of the Animals). Orchestral work.
Sibelius, Jean (1865–1957)
"The Swan of Tuonela" from *Four Legends.* Opus 22.
Orchestral work.
Tchaikovsky, Peter Ilyich (1840–1893)
*Lac des cygnes* (Swan Lake). Opus 20. Ballet.
Wagner, Richard (1813–1883)
*Lohengrin* (The knight of the swan). Opera.

## OTHERS

Delius, Frederick (1862–1934)
*Late Swallows.* String quartet.
Goodenberger, Jennifer (1957–
*Flight: A Bird Suite.* Violin and piano. Four movements:
(1) "Morninglarc" (2) "I Danced with the Phoenix"
(3) "Kisses of Aengus" (4) "Nightbird's Space Lullabye."
Haydn, Franz Joseph (1732–1809)
Quartet No. 39 in C major *Vogelquartett* (Bird quartet). Opus 33,
No. 3. String quartet.
Liadov, Anatol (1855–1914)
"Legend of the Birds" from *Eight Russian Folksongs.*
Opus 58. Orchestral work.
Liszt, Franz (1811–1886)
"St. François d'Assise prédicant aux oiseaux" (St. Francis of
Assisi's sermon to the birds) from *Légendes.* Piano.
MacDowell, Edward (1860–1908)
"Stork's Story" from *Moon Pictures.* Opus 21. Piano duet.
"The Eagle" from *Four Little Poems.* Opus 32. Piano.
"To a Hummingbird" from *Six Fancies.* Opus 7. Piano.
Malipiero, Gian Francesco (1882–1973)
*Impressioni dal vero* (Impressions from nature). Orchestral work.
Three movements: (1) "Il Capinero" (The blackcap)
(2) "Il Picchio" (The woodpecker) (3) "Il Chiù" (The owl).

Messiaen, Olivier (1908–
  "Abîme des oiseaux" (Abyss of the birds) from *Quatuor pour la fin
    du temps* (Quartet for the end of time). Clarinet, violin, cello,
    piano.
  "Amen of the Angels, of the Saints, of the Song of the Birds" from
    *Visions de l'amen*. Two pianos.
  *Oiseaux exotiques* (Exotic birds). Piano.
  *Réveil des oiseaux* (The awakening of the birds). Piano and
    orchestra.
Prokofiev, Sergei (1891–1953)
  Bird and Duck Motifs from *Peter and the Wolf*. Opus 67.
    Narrator and orchestra.
  *Ugly Duckling*. Opus 18. Orchestral work.
Rachmaninoff, Sergei (1873–1943)
  "The Sea and Seagulls" from *Etudes–Tableaux*. Opus 39, No. 2.
    Piano.
Rameau, Jean–Philippe (1683–1764)
  *Le Rappel des oiseaux* (The recall of the birds). Harpsichord.
Ravel, Maurice (1875–1937)
  "Oiseaux tristes" (Sad birds) from *Miroirs* (mirrors). Piano.
Respighi, Ottorino (1879–1936)
  *Gli Uccelli* (The birds). Orchestral work. Five movements:
    (1) "Preludio" (2) "La Colomba" (The dove) (3) "La Gallina"
    (The hen) (4) "L'Usignuolo" (The nightingale) (5) "Il Cucu"
    (The cuckoo).
Rossini, Gioacchino (1792–1868)
  *La Gazza ladra* (The thieving magpie). Opera.
Saint–Saëns, Camille (1835–1921)
  "The Aviary" from *Le Carnaval des animaux: fantaisie zoologique*
    (Carnival of the animals). Orchestral work.
Schumann, Robert (1810–1856)
  "Vogel als Prophet" (Bird as prophet) from *Waldenscenen* (Forest
    scenes). Opus 82, No. 7. Piano.
Stravinsky, Igor (1882–1971)
  *L'Oiseau de feu* (The firebird). Ballet.
Thomson, Virgil (1896–
  "Bugles and Birds (A portait of Pablo Picasso)" from *Portraits*.
    Album 1. Piano.
Villa–Lobos, Heitor (1887–1959)
  "Cloth Bird" from *Os animalinhos* (Little toy animals) from *Prole do
    bêbê* (Baby's playthings) No. 2. Piano.
  *Uirapurú* (The enchanted bird). Ballet.


BLACKS — see also Africa

Coleridge–Taylor, Samuel (1875–1912)
  *24 Negro Melodies*. Opus 59. Piano.

Dawson, William Levi (1898–
*Negro Folk Symphony.*
Dvořák, Antonín (1841–1904)
Symphony No. 9 in E minor *From the New World.* Opus 95.
Gershwin, George (1898–1937)
*Porgy and Bess.* Opera.
Gilbert, Henry F. (1868–1928)
*Comedy Overture on Negro Themes.* Orchestral work.
*Negro Dances.* Piano.
*Negro Rhapsody.* Orchestral work.
Goldmark, Rubin (1872–1936)
*Negro Rhapsody.* Orchestral work.
Powell, John (1882–1963)
*Rapsodie nègre* (Negro rhapsody). Piano and orchestra.
Still, William Grant (1895–1978)
*Afro–American Symphony.* Orchestral work.
*Darker America.* Orchestral work.
*In Memoriam: the Colored Soldiers who died for Democracy.*
Orchestral work.


BOATS — see Ships


BOHEMIA

Dvořák, Antonín (1841–1904)
*From the Bohemian Forest.* Opus 68. Piano duet. Six movements:
(1) "In the Spinning–Room" (2) "On the Dark Lake" (3) "Witches'
Sabbath" (4) "On the Watch" (5) "Silent Woods" (6) "In Troubled
Times."
*My Home.* Opus 62. Orchestral work.
Hadley, Henry (1871–1937)
*In Bohemia.* Opus 28. Orchestral work.
Novák, Vítezslav (1870–1949)
*South Bohemian Suite.* Opus 64. Orchestral work.
Smetana, Bedrich (1824–1884)
*Má Vlast* (My country). Orchestral work. Six movements:
(1) "Vysehrad" (2) "Vltava" (3) "Sárka" (4) "From Bohemia's
Fields and Groves" (5) "Tábor" (6) "Blaník."


BRAZIL — see also Latin America

Mignone, Francisco (1897–1986)
*Congada: dansa Afrobrasileira.* Orchestral work.

*Festa das igrejas* (Four churches). Orchestral work.
Milhaud, Darius (1892–1974)
   *Saudades do brasil* (Brazilian nostalgia). Opus 67. Piano;
     orchestral work. Twelve movements: (1) "Sorocabo"
     (2) "Botofogo" (3) "Leme" (4) "Copacabana" (5) "Ipanema"
     (6) "Gavea" (7) "Corcovado" (8) "Tijuca" (9) "Sumaré"
     (10) "Paineras" (11) "Laranjeiras" (12) "Paysandú." (Districts of
     Rio de Janeiro)
Respighi, Ottorino (1879–1936)
   *Impressioni brasiliane* (Brazilian impressions). Orchestral work.
     Three movements: (1) "Notte tropicale" (Tropical night)
     (2) "Butantan" (3) "Canzone e danza" (Song & dance).
Villa–Lobos, Heitor (1887–1959)
   *Bachianas brasileiras.* Nos. 1–9. Voice, piano, and/or orchestral
     works. (No. 1, for eight cellos; No. 2, for chamber orchestra;
     No. 3, for piano and orchestra; No. 4, for orchestra; No. 5, for
     voice and eight cellos; No. 6, for flute and basson; No. 7, for
     orchestra; No. 8, for orchestra; No. 9, for strings.)
   *Brazil.* Band.
   *Cirandinha.* Piano.
   Quartet No. 5 in E major *Brazilian.* String quartet.
   *Suite popular brasileira.* Guitar.


BUFFOONS — see Circus, Clowns


BUILDINGS — see also Castles, Church

Beethoven, Ludwig van (1770–1827)
   *Die Weihe des Hauses* (Consecration of the house). Opus 124.
     Orchestral work.
Carpenter, John Alden (1876–1951)
   *Skyscrapers: A Ballet of American Life.* Ballet.
Copland, Aaron (1900–
   "Skyline" from *Music for a Great City.* Orchestral work.
Debussy, Claude (1862–1918)
   "La Cathédrale engloutie" (The engulfed cathedral) from *Préludes I.*
     Piano.
   "La Puerta del vino" (The famous gate of Alhambra) from *Préludes II.*
     Piano.
   "Pagodes" (Pagodas) from *Estampes* (Engravings). Piano.
Glazunov, Alexander (1865–1936)
   *The Kremlin.* Opus 30. Orchestral work.
Mussorgsky, Modest (1839–1881)
   "The Great Gate of Kiev" from *Pictures at an Exhibition.* Piano;
     orchestral work.

Villa–Lobos, Heitor (1887–1959)
*New York Sky–Line Melody.* Orchestral work.


BUTTERFLY — see also Insects

Chopin, Frederic (1810–1849)
Étude No. 9 in G–flat major *The Butterfly.* Opus 25. Piano.
Couperin, François (1631–1701)
*Les Papillons* (Butterflies). Ordre 2, No. 22. Harpsichord.
Elgar, Edward (1857–1934)
"Moths and Butterflies" from *Wand of Youth Suite* No. 2. Opus
1b. Orchestral work.
Grieg, Edvard (1843–1907)
"Sommerfugl" (Butterfly) from *Lyric Pieces.* Opus 43, No. 1. Piano.
Puccini, Giacomo (1858–1924)
*Madama Butterfly.* Opera.
Roussel, Albert (1869–1937)
"Dance of the Butterfly" from *Le Festin de l'araignée* (The spider's
feast). Opus 17. Ballet.
Schumann, Robert (1810–1856)
"Papillons" (Butterflies) from *Carnaval.* Opus 9. Piano.


# C


CARNIVAL — see also Festivals

Berlioz, Hector (1803–1869)
*Le Carnaval romain* (Roman carnival). Opus 9.
Orchestral work.
Britten, Benjamin (1913–1976)
"Fun–Fair" from *Holiday Diary.* Opus 5. Piano.
Dvořák, Antonín (1841–1904)
*Carnival Overture.* Opus 92. Orchestral work.
Glazunov, Alexander (1865–1936)
*Carnival.* Opus 45. Orchestral work.
Grofé, Ferde (1892–1972)
"Mardi Gras" from *Mississippi Suite.* Orchestral work.

Saint–Saëns, Camille (1835–1921)
  *Le Carnaval des animaux: fantaisie zoologique* (Carnival of the animals:
  grand zoological fantasy). Orchestral work. Fourteen movements:
  (1) "Introduction and Royal Lions' March" (2) "Hens and Cocks"
  (3) "Hemiones – Swift Animals" (4) "Tortoises"
  (5) "The Elephant" (6) "Kangaroos" (7) "Aquarium"
  (8) "Long–eared Personages" (9) "The Cuckoo in the Depths of the
  Wood" (10) "The Aviary" (11) "Pianists" (12) "Fossils"
  (13) "The Swan" (14) "Finale."
Satie, Erik (1866–1925)
  "Le Carnaval" from *Sports et divertissements* (Sports and
  entertainments). Piano.
Schumann, Robert (1810–1856)
  *Carnaval.* Opus 9. Piano. Twenty movements:
  (1) "Préambule" (2) "Pierrot" (3) "Arlequin" (4) "Valse Noble"
  (5) "Eusebius" (6) "Florestan" (7) "Coquette" (8) "Réplique"
  (Reply) (Sphinxes) (9) "Papillons" (Butterflies)
  (10) "A.S.C.H. – S.C.H.A." (Lettres dansantes) (Dancing letters)
  (11) "Chiarina" (12) "Chopin" (13) "Estrella"
  (14) "Reconnaissance" (15) "Pantalon et Colombine"
  (16) "Valse Allemande; Intermezzo: Paganini" (17) "Aveu"
  (Confession) (18) "Promenade" (19) "Pause" (20) "Marche des
  'Davidsbündler' contre les Philistins" (March of the League of
  David against the Philistines).
  *Faschingsschwank aus Wien* (Carnival jest from Vienna).
  Opus 26. Piano.
Svendsen, Johan Severin (1840–1911)
  *Norwegian Artists' Carnival.* Opus 16. Orchestral work.
  *The Carnival in Paris.* Opus 9. Orchestral work.
Tchaikovsky, Peter Ilyich (1840–1893)
  "February: Carnival Time" from *The Seasons.* Opus 37b. Piano.
Tommasini, Vincenzo (1878–1950)
  *Il Carnevale di Venezia* (The carnival of Venice). Orchestral work.


CASTLES — see also Buildings

Bax, Arnold (1883–1953)
  *Tintagel.* Orchestral work.
Elgar, Edward (1857–1934)
  "The Queen's Tower at Night" from *King Arthur Suite.* Orchestral
  work.
Mussorgsky, Modest (1839–1881)
  "The Old Castle" from *Pictures at an Exhibition.* Piano;
  orchestral work.
Prokofiev, Sergei (1891–1953)
  "Cinderella and the Castle" from *Cinderella.* Opus 87, No. 2. Ballet.

Sibelius, Jean (1865–1957)
"At the Castle Gate" from *Pelléas et Mélisande.* Opus 46. Orchestral work.
Smetana, Bedrich (1824–1884)
"Vysehrad" from *Má Vlast* (My country). Orchestral work.
Turina, Joaquín (1882–1949)
"En la torre del castillo" (In the tower of the citadel) from *Sanlúcar de Barrameda.* Opus 24. Piano.

CATS — see also Animals

Bizet, Georges (1838–1875)
"Les Quatre coins" (Puss in the corner) from *Jeux d' enfants* (Games of children). Piano duet.
Chopin, Frederic (1810–1849)
Waltz in F major *Cat's Waltz.* Opus 34, No. 3. Piano.
Copland, Aaron (1900–
*The Cat and the Mouse.* Piano.
Fauré, Gabriel (1845–1924)
"Kitty–Valse" and "Mi–a–ou" from *Dolly Suite.* Opus 56. Piano duet.
Prokofiev, Sergei (1891–1953)
Cat motif from *Peter and the Wolf.* Opus 67. Narrator and orchestra.
Scarlatti, Domenico (1685–1757)
Sonata in G minor *Cat's Fugue.* L. 499. Harpsichord.
Villa–Lobos, Heitor (1887–1959)
"Cardboard Cat" from *Os animalinhos* (Little toy animals) from *Prole do bêbê* (Baby's playthings) No. 2. Piano.

CAUCASIAN

Balakirev, Mily (1837–1910)
*Islamey.* Piano.
Ippolitov–Ivanov, Mikhail (1859–1965)
*Caucasian Sketches.* Opus 10. Orchestral work. Four movements:
(1) "In the Pass" (2) "In the Village" (3) "In the Mosque"
(4) "The March of the Sardar."
Prokofiev, Sergei (1891–1953)
Quartet No. 2 in F major. Opus 92. String quartet.

# CELTIC

Bax, Arnold (1883–1953)
Quintet for oboe and string quartet.
Hill, Alfred (1870–1960)
Symphony No. 6 in B–flat major *Celtic*.
MacDowell, Edward (1860–1908)
Sonata No. 4 *Keltic*. Opus 59. Piano.
Rogowski, Ludomir (1881–1954)
*A Celtic Legend*. Orchestral work. Three movements: (1) "Solemn
Entrance of the Knights of the Round Table and the Oath of King
Arthur" (2) "The Dance of Vivian with the Spirits of Earth"
(3) "Sea–Crossing of Merlin."

# CHILDREN — see also Fairy Tales, Dolls, Marionettes and Puppets

Bartók, Béla (1881–1945)
"Children's Song" from *Mikrokosmos*. Book 4. Piano.
*For Children*. Piano.
Bizet, Georges (1838–1875)
*Jeux d'enfants* (Children's games). Piano duet. Twelve movements:
(1) "L'Escarpolette" (The swing) (2) "La Toupie" (The top)
(3) "La Poupée" (The doll) (4) "Les Chevaux de bois" (Wooden
horses) (5) "Le Volant" (Battledore and Shuttlecock)
(6) "Trompette et tambour" (Trumpet and drum) (7) "Les Bulles de
savon" (Soap bubbles) (8) "Les Quatre coins" (Puss in the corner)
(9) "Colin–maillard" (Blind–man's bluff) (10) "Saute–mouton"
(Leap–frog) (11) "Petit mari, petite femme" (Little husband, little
wife) (12) "Le Bal" (The ball).
Britten, Benjamin (1913–1976)
*Young Person's Guide to the Orchestra*. Narrator and orchestra.
Carpenter, John Alden (1876–1951)
*Adventures in a Perambulator*. Orchestral work. Six movements:
(1) "Take Your Seat" (2) "The Policeman" (3) "The Hurdy
Gurdy" (4) "The Lake" (5) "The Dogs" (6) "Dreams."
Debussy, Claude (1862–1918)
*Children's Corner*. Piano. Six movements: (1) "Doctor Gradus ad
Parnassum" (2) "Jimbo's Lullaby" (3) "Serenade for the Doll"
(4) "The Snow is Dancing" (5) "The Little Shepherd"
(6) "Golliwog's Cakewalk."
Dohnányi, Ernst von (1877–1960)
*Variations on a Nursery Song*. Opus 25. Piano and orchestra.
Elgar, Edward (1857–1934)
*Dream Children*. Opus 43. Orchestral work.

*Nursery Suite.* Opus 86. Orchestral work. Seven movements:
(1) "Aubade" (2) "The Serious Doll" (3) "Busy–ness"
(4) "The Sad Doll" (5) "The Wagon" (6) "The Merry Doll"
(7) "Dreaming–envoy."

*Wand of Youth Suite No. 1.* Opus 1a. Orchestral work.
Seven movements: (1) "Overture" (2) "Serenade" (3) "Minuet"
(4) "Sun Dance" (5) "Fairy Pipers" (6) "Slumber Scene"
(7) "Fairies and Giants."

*Wand of Youth Suite No. 2.* Opus 1b. Orchestral work.
Six movements: (1) "March" (2) "The Little Bells" (3) "Moths
and Butterflies" (4) "Fountain Dance" (5) "The Tame Bear"
(6) "The Wild Bears."

Grainger, Percy (1882–1961)
*Youthful Suite.* Orchestral work.

Hanson, Howard (1896–1981)
*Fantasy Variations on a Theme of Youth.* Orchestral work.

Harris, Roy (1898–1979)
*Children at Play.* Piano.
*Memories of a Child's Sunday.* Orchestral work.

MacDowell, Edward (1860–1908)
*Moon Pictures.* Opus 21. Piano duet. Five movements:
(1) "The Hindoo Maiden" (2) "Stork's Story" (3) "In Tyrol"
(4) "The Swan" (5) "Visit of the Bear." (Inspired by Hans
Christian Andersen.)

Mendelssohn, Felix (1809–1847)
*6 Kinderstücke* (Six children's pieces). "Christmas Pieces." Opus 72.
Piano.

Prokofiev, Sergei (1891–1953)
*Children's Suite.* Opus 65. Piano.

Ravel, Maurice (1875–1937)
*Ma Mère l'Oye* (Mother Goose suite). Orchestral work; piano duet.
Five movements: (1) "Pavane de la belle au bois dormant" (Pavane
of Sleeping Beauty) (2) "Petit Poucet" (Tom Thumb)
(3) "Laideronette, impératrice des pagodas" (Little ugly one,
empress of the pagodas) (4) "Les Entretiens de la belle et la bête"
(Conversations with beauty and the beast) (5) "Le Jardin féerique"
(The fairy garden).

Schumann, Robert (1810–1856)
*Album für die Jugend* (Album for the young). Opus 68. Piano.

*Kinderscenen* (Scenes from childhood). Opus 15. Piano.
Thirteen movements: (1) "Von fremden Ländern und Menschen"
(From foreign lands) (2) "Kuriose Geschichte" (Funny story)
(3) "Hasche–Mann" (Catch me if you can) (4) "Bittendes Kind"
(Entreating child) (5) "Glückes genug" (Quite happy)
(6) "Wichtige Begebenheit" (Important event) (7) "Träumerei"
(Dreaming) (8) "Am Kamin" (At the fireside) (9) "Ritter vom
Steckenpferd" (Knight of the hobby–horse) (10) "Fast zu ernst"
(Almost too serious) (11) "Fürchtenmachen" (Frightening)
(12) "Kind im Einschlummern" (Child falling asleep)
(13) "Der Dichter spricht" (The poet speaks).
Tchaikovsky, Peter Ilyich (1840–1893)
*Nutcracker Suite.* Opus 71a. Ballet. Eight movements:
(1) "Overture" (2) "March" (3) "Dance of the Sugarplum Fairy"
(4) "Russian Dance" (5) "Arabian Dance" (6) "Chinese Dance"
(7) "Dance of the Flutes" (8) "Waltz of the Flowers."
Villa–Lobos, Heitor (1887–1959)
*Prole do bêbê* (Baby's playthings).
*A familia do bêbê* (Dolls). No. 1. Piano. Eight movements:
(1) "Porcelain" (2) "Paper" (3) "Clay" (4) "Rubber"
(5) "Wooden" (6) "Rag" (7) "Punch" (8) "Witch Doll."
*Os animalinhos* (Little toy animals). No. 2. Piano.
Eight movements: (1) "Cardboard Cat" (2) "Toy Mouse"
(3) "Rubber Dog" (4) "Wooden Horse" (5) "Tin Ox"
(6) "Cloth Bird" (7) "Cotton Bean" (8) "Glass Wolf."
Zádor, Eugene (1894–1977)
*Children's Symphony.* Four movements: (1) "Allegro moderato"
(2) "Fairy Tale" (3) "Scherzo militaire" (4) "The Farm."


# CHINA

Bartók, Béla (1881–1945)
*The Miraculous Mandarin.* Opus 19. Ballet.
Chasins, Abram (1903–
*Three Chinese Pieces.* Orchestral work. Three movements:
(1) "A Shanghai Tragedy" (2) "Flirtation in a Chinese Garden"
(3) "Rush Hour in Hong Kong."
Debussy, Claude (1862–1918)
"Pagode" from *Estampes.* Piano.
Glière, Reinhold (1875–1956)
*The Red Poppy.* Opus 70. Ballet.
Griffes, Charles Tomlinson (1884–1920)
*Pleasure Dome of Kubla Khan.* Orchestral work.
Ketelbey, Albert (1875–1959)
*In a Chinese Temple Garden.* Orchestral work.
Puccini, Giacomo (1858–1924)
*Turandot.* Opera.

Stravinsky, Igor (1882–1971)
  *Le Chant du rossignol* (The song of the nightingale). Ballet;
    orchestral work. Three movements: (1) "The Palace of the Chinese
    Emperor" (2) "The Two Nightingales" (3) "Illness and Recovery
    of the Chinese Emperor."
  *Le Rossignol* (The nightingale). Opera.
Tchaikovsky, Peter Ilyich (1840–1893)
  "Chinese Dance" from *Nutcracker Suite*. Opus 71a. Ballet.


CHRIST — see also Bible, Christmas, Easter, Jewish, Religious Figures

Bach, Johann Sebastian (1685–1750)
  "Jesu, Joy of Man's Desiring" from *Cantata 147*. Instrumental
    arrangements.
Creston, Paul (1906–1985)
  Symphony No. 3 *Three Mysteries*. Opus 48. Three movements:
    (1) "The Nativity" (2) "The Crucifixion" (3) "The Resurrection."
Haydn, Franz Joseph (1732–1809)
  *Die Sieben Worte des Erlösers am Kreuze* (The seven last words of
    the saviour on the cross). Orchestral work.
Mahler, Gustav (1860–1911)
  Symphony No. 2 in C minor *Resurrection*.
Messiaen, Olivier (1908–
  "Amen of the Agony of Jesus" from *Visions de l'amen*. Two pianos.
  *L'Ascension* (The ascension). Orchestral work. Four movements:
    (1) "Majesty of Christ Beseeching His Glory of His Father"
    (2) "Serene Hallelujahs of a Soul that Longs for Heaven"
    (3) "Hallelujah on the Trumpet, Hallelujah on the Cymbal"
    (4) "Prayer of Christ Ascending to His Father."
  *La Nativité du Seigneur* (Birth of the Lord). Organ.
  *Les Offrandes oubliées* (Forgotten offerings). Orchestral work.
  "Louange à l'éternité de Jésus" (Praise to the eternity of Jesus) and
    "Louange à l'immortalité de Jésus" (Praise to the immortality of
    Jesus) from *Quatuor pour la fin du temps* (Quartet for the end
    of time). Clarinet, violin, cello, piano.
  *Vingt regards sur l'enfant Jésus* (Twenty views of Jesus the infant).
    Piano.
Respighi, Ottorino (1879–1936)
  "La Fuga in Egitto" (The flight into Egypt) from *Vetrate di chiesa*
    (Church windows). Orchestral work.
Schuman, William (1910–
  "When Jesus Wept" from *New England Triptych* (Three pieces for
    orchestra after William Billings).

CHRISTMAS — see also Christ, Easter

Barber, Samuel (1910–1981)
*Die Natali* (Christmastide). Opus 37. Orchestral work.
Bax, Arnold (1883–1953)
*Christmas Eve on the Mountains*. Orchestral work.
Corelli, Arcangelo (1653–1713)
Concerto Grosso No. 8 in G minor *Christmas Concerto*. Opus 6,
No. 8. Orchestral work.
Haydn, Franz Joseph (1732–1809)
Symphony No. 26 in D minor *Weihnachtssymphonie* (Christmas
symphony).
Liadov, Anatol (1855–1914)
"Christmas Carol" from *Eight Russian Folksongs*. Opus 58.
Orchestral work.
Manfredini, Francesco (1680–1748)
Concerto Grosso *Christmas Concerto*. Opus 3, No. 12. Orchestral
work.
Menotti, Gian Carlo (1911–
*Amahl and the Night Visitors*. Opera.
Mendelssohn, Felix (1809–1847)
*6 Kinderstücke* (Six children's pieces). "Christmas Pieces." Opus 72.
Piano.
Persichetti, Vincent (1915–
*Appalachian Christmas Carols*. Piano duet.
Respighi, Ottorino (1879–1936)
"L'Adorazione dei Magi" (Adoration of the Magi) from
*Trittico botticelliano* (Botticellian triptych). Orchestral work.
"La Befana" (The eve of the Epiphany in Piazza Navona) from *Feste
romane* (Roman festivals). Orchestral work.
Rimsky–Korsakov, Nikolai (1844–1908)
*Christmas Eve*. Opera.
Scott, Cyril (1879–1970)
*Christmas Overture*. Orchestral work.
Tchaikovsky, Peter Ilyich (1840–1893)
"December: Christmas" from *The Seasons*. Opus 37a. Piano.
*Nutcracker Suite*. Opus 71a. Ballet. Eight movements:
(1) "Overture" (2) "March" (3) "Dance of the Sugarplum Fairy"
(4) "Russian Dance" (5) "Arabian Dance" (6) "Chinese Dance"
(7) "Dance of the Flutes" (8) "Waltz of the Flowers."
Torelli, Giuseppe (1658–1709)
Concerto Grosso *Christmas Concerto*. Opus 8, No. 6. Two violins
and orchestra.
Vaughan Williams, Ralph (1872–1958)
*On Christmas Night*. Ballet.
Weinberger, Jaromir (1896–1967)
*Christmas*. Orchestral work.
Zádor, Eugene (1894–1977)
*A Christmas Overture*. Orchestral work.

CHURCH — see also Buildings

Debussy, Claude (1862–1918)
"La Cathédrale engloutie" (The engulfed cathedral) from *Préludes I*. Piano.
Dello Joio, Norman (1913–
"The Cloisters" from *New York Profiles*. Orchestral work.
Ibert, Jacques (1890–1962)
"A Paris Mosque" from *Paris*. Orchestral work.
Ippolitov–Ivanov, Mikhail (1859–1965)
"In the Mosque" from *Caucasian Sketches*. Opus 10. Orchestral work.
Ives, Charles (1874–1954)
*From the Steeples and the Mountains*. Orchestral work.
Ketelbey, Albert (1875–1959)
*In a Monastery Garden*. Orchestral work.
Mignone, Francisco (1897–1986)
*Festa das igrejas* (Four churches). Orchestral work.
Respighi, Ottorino (1879–1936)
*Vetrate di chiesa* (Church windows). Orchestral work.
Four movements: (1) "La Fuga in Egitto" (The flight into Egypt)
(2) "San Michele Arcangelo" (The archangel Michael)
(3) "Mattutino di Santa Chiara" (The Matin of Saint Claire)
(4) "San Gregorio Magno" (St. Gregory the Great).

CIRCUS — see also Clowns

Copland, Aaron (1900–
"Circus March" from *The Red Pony*. Orchestral work.
Leoncavallo, Ruggero (1857–1919)
*I Pagliacci* (The buffoons). Opera.
Moore, Douglas (1893–1969)
*The Pageant of P.T. Barnum*. Orchestral work. Five movements:
(1) "Boyhood at Bethal" (2) "Joice Heth" (3) "General & Mrs. Tom Thumb" (4) "Jenny Lind" (5) "Circus Parade."
Piston, Walter (1894–1976)
"Arrival of Circus" and "Circus March" from *The Incredible Flutist*. Orchestral work.
Respighi, Ottorino (1879–1936)
"Circenses" (The circus maximus) from *Feste romane* (Roman festivals). Orchestral work.
Schuman, William (1910–
*Circus Overture* (Side show). Orchestral work.
Stravinsky, Igor (1882–1971)
*Polka for Circus Elephants*. Orchestral work.

Taylor, Deems (1885–1966)
*Circus Day Suite.* Orchestral work.
Toch, Ernst (1887–1964)
*Circus Overture.* Orchestral work.


# CITIES

## GREEK

Beethoven, Ludwig van (1770–1827)
*Die Ruinen von Athen* (The ruins of Athens). Opus 113.
Orchestral work.
Rossini, Gioacchino (1792–1868)
*L'Assedio di Corinto* (The siege of Corinth). Opera.

## LONDON

Elgar, Edward (1857–1934)
*Cockaigne* (In London town.) Opus 40. Orchestral work.
Haydn, Franz Joseph (1732–1809)
Symphony No. 104 in D major *London.*
Ireland, John (1879–1962)
*A London Overture.* Orchestral work.
*London Pieces.* Piano. Three movements: (1) "Chelsea Reach"
(2) "Ragamuffin" (3) "Soho Forenoons."
Vaughan Williams, Ralph (1872–1958)
*A London Symphony.*

## NEW YORK

Bernstein, Leonard (1918–
*On the Town.* Orchestral work.
Copland, Aaron (1900–
*Music for a Great City.* Orchestral work. Four movements:
(1) "Skyline" (2) "Night Thoughts" (3) "Subway Jam"
(4) Toward the Bridge."
Dello Joio, Norman (1913–
*New York Profiles.* Orchestral work. Four movements:
(1) "The Cloisters" (2) "The Park" (3) "The Tomb" (4) "Little
Italy."
Ives, Charles (1874–1954)
*Central Park in the Dark.* Chamber orchestra.
Siegmeister, Elie (1909–
*Sunday in Brooklyn.* Orchestral work.
Thomson, Virgil (1896–
*The Mayor La Guardia Waltzes.* Orchestral work.

Whithorne, Emerson (1884–1958)
*New York Days and Nights*. Piano.

## PARIS

Delius, Frederick (1862–1934)
*Paris: The Song of a Great City*. Orchestral work.
Gershwin, George (1898–1937)
*An American in Paris*. Orchestral work.
Haydn, Franz Joseph (1732–1809)
Symphonies *Paris*. Opuses 82, 83, 84, 85, 86, 87.
Ibert, Jacques (1890–1962)
*Paris*. Orchestral work. Six movements: (1) "The Métro"
(2) "A Suburb" (3) "A Paris Mosque" (4) "A Restaurant in the
Bois–de–Boulogne" (5) "The Steamer" (6) "The Fair."
Milhaud, Darius (1892–1974)
*Paris*. Four pianos. Six movements: (1) "Montmartre"
(2) "L'Ile Saint–Louis" (3) "Montparnasse"
(4) "Bateaux–mouches" (5) "Longchamps" (6) "La Tour
Eiffel."
Mozart, Wolfgang Amadeus (1756–1791)
Symphony No. 31 in D major *Paris*. K. 297.
Offenbach, Jacques (1819–1880)
*Gaîté parisienne*. Ballet.
Svendsen, Johan Severin (1840–1911)
*The Carnival in Paris*. Opus 9. Orchestral work.

## POLISH

Addinsell, Richard (1904–1977)
*Warsaw Concerto*. Piano and orchestra.
Mozart, Wolfgang Amadeus (1756–1791)
Symphony No. 36 in C major *Linz*. K. 425.
Symphony No. 38 in D major *Prague*. K. 504.

## ROME

Berlioz, Hector (1803–1869)
*Le Carnaval romain* (Roman carnival). Opus 9.
Orchestral work.
Griffes, Charles Tomlinson (1884–1920)
*Four Roman Sketches*. Opus 7. Piano; orchestral work.
Four movements: (1) "The White Peacock" (2) "Nightfall"
(3) "The Fountain of Acqua Paola" (4) "Clouds."
Ibert, Jacques (1890–1962)
"Rome–Palerme" from *Escales* (Ports). Orchestral work.

Respighi, Ottorino (1879–1936)
*Feste romane* (Roman festivals). Orchestral work.
Four movements: (1) "Circenses" (The circus maximus)
(2) "Il Giubilco" (The jubilee) (3) "L'Ottobrata" (The October
excursions) (4) "La Befana" (The eve of the Epiphany in Piazza
Navona."
*Fontane di Roma* (Fountains of Rome). Orchestral work.
Four movements: (1) "La Fontana di Valle Giulia all' alba" (The
fountain of Valle Giulia at dawn) (2) "La Fontana del Tritone al
mattino" (The fountain at Triton in the morning) (3) "La
Fontana di Trevi al meriggio" (The fountain of Trevi at midday)
(4) "La Fontana di Villa Medici al tramonto" (The fountain of the
Villa Medici at dusk).
*Pini di Roma* (Pines of Rome). Orchestral work.
Four movements: (1) "I Pini di Villa Borghese" (The pines of
the Villa Borghese) (2) "Pini presso una catacombe" (The pines
near a catacomb) (3) "I Pini del Gianicolo" (The pines of the
Janiculum) (4) "I Pini di Via Appia" (The pines of the Appian
Way).

SOVIET

Glazunov, Alexander (1865–1936)
*The Kremlin*. Opus 30. Orchestral work.
Prokofiev, Sergei (1891–1953)
Sonata No. 7 in B–flat major *Stalingrad*. Opus 83. Piano.
Shostakovich, Dmitri (1906–1975)
Symphony No. 7 *Leningrad*. Opus 60.

SPANISH

Albéniz, Isaac (1860–1909)
*Iberia*. Book I. "Evocación," "El Puerto" (The port), "El Corpus
Christie en Sevilla" or "Fête–Dieu à Séville" (Festival in
Seville). Piano.
*Iberia*. Book II. "Rondeña," "Almería," "Triana." Piano.
*Iberia*. Book III. "El Albaicín," "El Polo," "Lavapies." Piano.
*Iberia*. Book IV. "Málaga," "Jérez," "Eritaña." Piano.
*Suite española* (Spanish suite). Opus 47. Piano.
Eight movements: (1) "Granada" (2) "Cataluña" (3) "Sevilla"
(4) "Cádiz" (5) "Asturias" (6) "Aragón" (7) "Casilla"
(8) "Cuba."
Debussy, Claude (1862–1918)
"Soirée dans Grenade" (Evening party in Granada) from *Estampes*
(Engravings). Piano.
Glinka, Mikhail (1804–1857)
*Summer Night in Madrid*. Orchestral work.

Ibert, Jacques (1890–1962)
  "Valencia" from *Escales* (Ports). Orchestral work.
Turina, Joaquín (1882–1949)
  *Sevilla.* Opus 2. Piano. Three movements: (1) "Sous les
  orangers" (Under the orange trees) (2) "Le Jeudi saint à minuit"
  (Holy Thursday at midnight) (3) "La Feria" (Holiday).

## VENICE

Pizzetti, Ildebrando (1880–1968)
  *Rondo veneziano.* Orchestral work.
Salieri, Antonio (1750–1825)
  Symphony in D major *Veneziana.*
Tommasini, Vincenzo (1878–1950)
  *Il Carnevale di Venezia* (The carnival of Venice). Orchestral work.

## VIENNA

Schumann, Robert (1810–1856)
  *Faschingsschwank aus Wien* (Carnival jest from Vienna).
  Opus 26. Piano.
Strauss, Johann Jr. (1825–1899)
  *Wiener Blut* (Vienna blood). Opus 354. Waltz.

## OTHERS

Copland, Aaron (1900–
  *Our Town.* Orchestral work.
  *Quiet City.* Orchestral work.
Chasins, Abram (1903–
  "A Shanghai Tragedy" and "Rush Hour in Hong Kong" from
  *Three Chinese Pieces.* Orchestral work.
Grofé, Ferde (1892–1972)
  *Metropolis.* Orchestral work.
Ibert, Jacques (1890–1962)
  *Escales* (Ports). Orchestral work. Three movements:
    (1) "Rome–Palerme" (2) "Tunis–Nefia" (3) "Valencia."
Ives, Charles (1874–1954)
  Sonata No. 2 *Concord.* Piano. Four movements: (1) "Emerson"
    (2) "Hawthorne" (3) "The Alcotts" (4) "Thoreau."
Liszt, Franz (1811–1886)
  "Les Cloches de Genève" (The bells of Geneva) from *Années de
    pèlerinage: Première année: Suisse* (Years of pilgrimage: first
    year: Switzerland). Piano.

Milhaud, Darius (1892–1974)
  *Saudades do brasil* (Brazilian nostalgia). Opus 67. Piano;
    orchestral work.  Twelve movements: (1) "Sorocabo"
    (2) "Botofogo" (3) "Leme" (4) "Copacabana" (5) "Ipanema"
    (6) "Gavea" (7) "Corcovado" (8) "Tijuca" (9) "Sumaré"
    (10) "Paineras" (11) "Laranjeiras" (12) "Paysandú." (Districts
    of Rio de Janeiro.)
Revueltas, Silvestre (1899–1940)
  *Cuauhnahuac* (Cuernavaca). Orchestral work.
Rimsky–Korsakov, Nikolai (1844–1908)
  "Festival at Bagdad" from *Scheherazade.* Opus 35. Orchestral
    work.
Tchaikovsky, Peter Ilyich (1840–1893)
  Sextet *Souvenir de Florence* (Recollection of Florence). Opus 70.
    String sextet.


CLOCK — see also Bells

Anderson, Leroy (1908–1975)
  *The Syncopated Clock.* Orchestral work.
Couperin, François (1631–1701)
  *Le Réveil–matin* (The alarm clock). Ordre 4, No. 4.
    Harpsichord.
  *Le Tic–toc–choc* (The ticking clock). Ordre 18, No. 6.
    Harpsichord.
Haydn, Franz Joseph (1732–1809)
  Symphony No. 101 in D major *Clock.*
Ketelbey, Albert (1875–1959)
  *The Clock and the Dresden Figures.* Orchestral work.
Kodály, Zoltán (1882–1967)
  "The Viennese Musical Clock" from *Háry János.* Orchestral work.
Toch, Ernst (1887–1964)
  *Big Ben.* Opus 62. Orchestral work.


CLOTHING

Couperin, François (1631–1701)
  *Le Bavolet flotant* (The floating bonnet). Ordre 9, No. 8.
    Harpsichord.
Falla, Manuel de (1876–1946)
  *El Sombrero de tres picos* (The three–cornered hat). Ballet.
Moore, Douglas (1893–1969)
  "Sunday Clothes" from *Farm Journal.* Chamber orchestra.

Strauss, Richard (1864–1949)
"Dance of the Seven Veils" from *Salome*. Orchestral work.
Tcherepnin, Alexander (1899–1977)
"Veils and Daggers" from *Georgiana*. Opus 92. Piano and strings.
Turina, Joaquín (1882–1949)
"Siluetas de la calzada" (Portrait of a woman in shoes) from
*Sanlúcar de Barrameda*. Opus 24. Piano.


CLOUDS — see also Weather

Debussy, Claude (1862–1918)
"Nuages" (Clouds) from *Nocturnes*. Orchestral work.
Griffes, Charles Tomlinson (1884–1920)
"Clouds" from *Four Roman Sketches*. Opus 7. Piano; orchestral
work.
Grofé, Ferde (1892–1972)
"Cloudburst" from *Grand Canyon Suite*. Orchestral work.
Haydn, Franz Joseph (1732–1809)
Quartet No. 82 in F major *Wait till the Clouds Roll By*.
Opus 77, No. 2. String quartet.
MacDowell, Edward (1860–1908)
"Silver Clouds" from *Six Idyls after Goethe*. Opus 28. Piano.


CLOWNS — see also Circus

Bantock, Granville (1868–1946)
*The Pierrot of the Minute*. Orchestral work.
Busoni, Ferruccio (1866–1924)
*Rondo arlecchinesco*. Opus 46. Orchestral work.
Kabalevsky, Dmitri (1904–1987)
*The Comedians*. Opus 26. Orchestral work.
Leoncavallo, Ruggero (1857–1919)
*I Pagliacci* (The buffoons). Opera.
Prokofiev, Sergei (1891–1953)
*Chout* (Buffoon). Opus 21. Ballet. Twelve movements:
(1) "The Clown and his Wife" (2) "Dance of the Buffoon's Wife"
(3) "The Buffoons Kill their Wives" (4) "The Buffoon
Masquerades as a Young Girl" (5) "Third Entr'acte" (6) "Dance of
the Buffoon's Daughters" (7) "The Arrival of the Merchant, Dance
of the Obeisance, and Choice of the Fiancée" (8) "In the Bedroom
of the Merchant" (9) "The Young Girl is Transformed into a Goat"
(10) "Fifth Entr'acte and Burial of the Goat" (11) "The Quarrel of
the Buffoon and the Merchant" (12) "Final Dance."

Reger, Max (1873–1916)
   "Colombine," "Harlequin," and "Pierrot und Pierrette" from *Ballet
   Suite*. Opus 130. Orchestral work.
Rimsky–Korsakov, Nikolai (1844–1908)
   "Dance of the Buffoons" from *The Snow Maiden*. Orchestral work.
Schumann, Robert (1810–1856)
   "Arlequin," "Pantalon et Colombine" and "Pierrot" from *Carnaval*.
   Opus 9. Piano.
Smetana, Bedrich (1824–1884)
   "Dance of the Comedians" from *The Bartered Bride*. Orchestral work.
Verdi, Giuseppe (1813–1901)
   *Rigoletto*. Opera.
Walton, William (1902–1983)
   *Scapino*. Orchestral work.


COAST — see also Ocean

Mendelssohn, Felix (1809–1847)
   *The Hebrides*. (Fingal's cave). Opus 26. Orchestral work.
Piston, Walter (1894–1976)
   "Seaside" from *Three New England Sketches*. Orchestral work.
Turina, Joaquín (1882–1949)
   "La Playe" (The beach) from *Sanlúcar de Barramada*. Opus 24.
   Piano.


## COLOR

Bliss, Arthur (1891–1975)
   *Colour Symphony*. Four Movements: (1) "Purple" (2) "Red"
   (3) "Blue" (4) "Green."
Bloch, Ernest (1880–1959)
   *Five Sketches in Sepia*. Piano.
Debussy, Claude (1862–1918)
   *En blanc et noir*. (In black and white). Two pianos.
Gershwin, George (1898–1937)
   *Rhapsody in Blue*. Piano and orchestra.
Grofé, Ferde (1892–1972)
   *Three Shades of Blue*. Orchestral work.
Purcell, Henry (1659–1695)
   Sonata No. 9 in F major *Golden*. Two violins and continuo.
Slonimsky, Nicolas (1894–
   *Studies in Black and White*. Piano.
Stravinsky, Igor (1882–1971)
   *Ebony Concerto*. Clarinet and orchestra.

Tchaikovsky, Peter Ilyich (1840–1893)
"Lilac Fairy" from *La Belle au bois dormant* (Sleeping beauty). Opus 66. Ballet.


## COMEDY — see also Clowns, Jokes

Chadwick, George (1854–1931)
*Thalia* (Muse of comedy). Orchestral work.


## CONVERSATION

Granados, Enrique (1867–1916)
"Coloquio en la reja" (Conversation through the grilled window) from *Goyescas*. Piano.
Ives, Charles (1874–1954)
"Discussions" and "Arguments" from *String Quartet No. 2*.


## COUNTRYSIDE — see also Earth

Beethoven, Ludwig van (1770–1827)
"The Awakening of Joyful Feelings upon Arrival in the Country" from Symphony No. 6 in F major *Pastoral*. Opus 68.
Berlioz, Hector (1803–1869)
"Scene in the Country" from *Symphonie fantastique* (Fantastic symphony). Opus 14.
Copland, Aaron (1900–
*An Outdoor Overture*. Orchestral work.
*The Tender Land*. Opera.
Cowell, Henry (1897–1965)
*Tales of our Countryside*. Piano and orchestra. Four movements: (1) "Deep Tides" (2) "Exultation" (3) "The Harp of Life" (4) "Country Reel."
Delius, Frederick (1862–1934)
*North Country Sketches*. Orchestral work. Four movements: (1) "Autumn – The Wind Soughs in the Trees" (2) "Winter Landscape" (3) "Dance" (4) "The March of Spring – Woodlands, Meadows and Silent Moors."
Schumann, Robert (1810–1856)
"Freundliche Landschaft" (Friendly countryside) from *Waldscenen* (Forest scenes). Opus 82. Piano.

## COWBOYS and COWGIRLS — see also Occupations, Prairie

Copland, Aaron (1900–
  *Billy the Kid.* Ballet; orchestral suite. Five movements:
    (1) "The Open Prairie" (2) "Street in Frontier Town" (3) "Card
    Game at Night" (4) "Gun Battle after Billy's Capture"
    (5) "The Open Prairie Again."
  *Rodeo.* Ballet; orchestral suite. Four movements: (1) "Buckaroo
    Holiday" (2) "Corral Nocturne" (3) "Saturday Night Waltz"
    (4) "Hoe Down."
Puccini, Giacomo (1858–1924)
  *La Fancialla del west* (The girl of the golden west). Opera.


## CREATION

Messiaen, Olivier (1908–
  "Amen of the Creation" from *Visions de l'amen.* Two pianos.
Milhaud, Darius (1892–1974)
  *La Création du monde* (The creation of the world). Ballet.


## CREOLE

Gilbert, Henry F. (1868–1928)
  *Dance in Plance Congo.* Orchestral work.
Ginastera, Alberto (1916–1983)
  *Creole Dance Suite.* Orchestral work.
Gottschalk, Louis Moreau (1829–1869)
  *Creole Ballads.* Piano.
Grofé, Ferde (1892–1972)
  "Old Creole Days" from *Mississippi Suite.* Orchestral work.


## CUBA

Caturla, Alejandro Garcia (1906–1940)
  *Primera suite cubana.* Piano and 8 wind instruments.
  *3 Danzas cubanas* (Three Cuban dances). Orchestral work.
Copland, Aaron (1900–
  *Danzon cubano.* Two pianos.
Gershwin, George (1898–1937)
  *Cuban Overture.* Orchestral work.

Gottschalk, Louis Moreau (1829–1869)
*Cuban Dances.* Piano.
Sanjuan, Pedro (1886–1976)
*Cuban Dance Suite* (Liturgia Negra). Orchestral work.

# D

## DANCE

Berlioz, Hector (1803–1869)
"Le Bal" (The ball) from *Symphonie fantastique* (Fantastic symphony). Opus 14.
Hindemith, Paul (1895–1963)
*1922.* Opus 26. Piano. Five movements: (1) "Marsch" (March) (2) "Schimmy" (3) "Nachtstück" (Night piece) (4) "Boston" (5) "Ragtime."
Poulenc, Francis (1899–1963)
*Le Bal masqué* (The masked ball). Chamber music.
Prokofiev, Sergei (1891–1953)
"Cinderella Dreams of the Ball" and "Dancing Lessons and Gavotte" from *Cinderella.* Opus 87, No. 2. Orchestral work.
"Cinderella Goes to the Ball" and "Cinderella's Waltz" from *Cinderella.* Opus 87, No. 1. Orchestral work.
Ravel, Maurice (1875–1937)
*La Valse* (The waltz). Orchestral work.
Reger, Max (1873–1916)
*Ballet Suite.* Opus 130. Orchestral work. Six movements: (1) "Entrée" (2) "Colombine" (3) "Harlequin" (4) "Pierrot und Pierrette" (5) "Valse d'amour" (6) "Finale."
Schelling, Ernest (1876–1939)
*A Victory Ball.* Orchestral work.
Stravinsky, Igor (1882–1971)
*Agon.* Ballet.
*Scénes de ballet* (Ballet scenes). Orchestral work. Eleven parts: (1) Introduction (2) Corps de Ballet Dances (3) Variation of the Ballerina (4) Pantomime (5) Pas de Deux (6) Pantomime (7) Variation of the Dancer (8) Variation of the Ballerina (9) Pantomime (10) Corps de Ballet Dances (11) Apotheosis.
Weber, Carl Maria von (1786–1826)
*Invitation to the Dance.* Opus 65. Orchestral work.

DAY — see also Afternoon, Evening, Morning, Night, Noon, Sunrise, Sunset

Indy, Vincent d' (1851–1931)
*Jour d'été à la montagne* (Summer day on the mountain). Opus 61. Piano and orchestra. Three movements: (1) "L'Aube" (Dawn) (2) "Le Jour" (Day) (3) "Le Soir" (Evening).
Prokofiev, Sergei (1891–1953)
*Summer Day*. Opus 65a. Orchestral work. Seven movements: (1) "Morning" (2) "Tag" (3) "Waltz" (4) "Regrets" (5) "March" (6) "Evening" (7) "Moonlit Meadows."


DEATH — see also Funeral, Tomb

Berg, Alban (1885–1935)
Concerto for Violin and Orchestra.
Berlioz, Hector (1803–1869)
"March to the Gallows" from *Symphonie fantastique* (Fantastic symphony). Opus 14.
Bliss, Arthur (1891–1975)
"Death of the Red Knight" from *Checkmate*. Ballet.
Busoni, Ferruccio (1866–1924)
*Berceuse élégiaque*. Opus 42. Orchestral work.
Chopin, Frederic (1810–1849)
Sonata No. 2 in B–flat major. Opus 35. Piano.
Elgar, Edward (1857–1934)
"Arthur's Passage to Avalon" from *King Arthur Suite*. Orchestral work.
Fauré, Gabriel (1845–1924)
"The Death of Mélisande" from *Pelléas et Mélisande*. Opus 80. Orchestral work.
Granados, Enrique (1867–1916)
"El Amor y la muerte" (Love and death) from *Goyescas*. Piano.
Grieg, Edvard (1843–1907)
"Ase's Death" from *Peer Gynt*. Opus 46. Orchestral work.
Huber, Hans (1852–1921)
Symphony No. 3. Opus 118.
Kuhnau, Johann (1660–1722)
"Hezekiah, Sick unto Death and Restored to Health" and "Jacob's Death and Burial" from *Biblical Sonatas*. Harpsichord.
Liszt, Franz (1811–1886)
*Totentanz (Danse macabre )* (Dance of death). Piano and orchestra.
Madetoja, Leevi (1887–1947)
*Kuoleman puutarha* (The garden of death). Opus 41. Piano.
Mussorgsky, Modest (1839–1881)
"Catacombs" from *Pictures at an Exhibition*. Piano; orchestral work.

Prokofiev, Sergei (1891–1953)
    "Juliet's Death" from *Romeo and Juliet*. Opus 101. Orchestral work.
    "Romeo at Juliet's Grave" from *Romeo and Juliet*. Opus 64–ter.
    Orchestral work.
    "The Death of Tybalt" from *Romeo and Juliet*. Opus 64–bis.
    Orchestral work.
Rachmaninoff, Sergei (1873–1943)
    *Toteninsel* (Isle of the dead). Opus 29. Orchestral work.
Ravel, Maurice (1875–1937)
    *Le Tombeau de Couperin* (The grave of Couperin). Orchestral work.
    *Pavane pour une infante défunte* (Pavane for a dead princess).
    Orchestral work.
Reger, Max (1873–1916)
    "Die Toteninsel" (Isle of the dead) from *Vier Tondichtungen nach
    Arnold Böcklin* (Four tone poems after Arnold Böcklin). Opus
    128. Orchestral work.
Saint–Saëns, Camille (1835–1921)
    *Danse macabre.* Opus 40. Orchestral work.
Schubert, Franz (1797–1828)
    Quartet No. 14 in D minor *Der Tod und das Mädchen* (Death and the
    maiden). String quartet.
Sibelius, Jean (1865–1957)
    "Death of Mélisande" from *Pelléas et Mélisande.* Opus 46.
    Orchestral work.
    "The Swan of Tuonela" from *Four Legends.* Opus 22. Orchestral
    work.
    *Valse triste.* Opus 44. Orchestral work.
Strauss, Richard (1864–1949)
    "The Hero's Escape from the World" from *Ein Heldenleben* (A hero's
    life). Opus 40. Orchestral work.
    *Tod und Verklärung* (Death and transfiguration). Opus 24. Orchestral
    work.
Wagner, Richard (1813–1883)
    "Brünnhilde's Immolation" and "Siegfried's Tod" (Siegfried's death)
    from *Götterdämmerung* (Twilight of the Gods). Orchestral work.
    "Vorspiel und Liebestod" (Prelude and love–death) from *Tristan und
    Isolde.* Orchestral work.


# DENMARK

Nielsen, Carl (1865–1931)
    *Journey to the Faroe Islands.* Orchestral work.
Saint–Saëns, Camille (1835–1921)
    *Caprice on Danish and Russian Airs.* Opus 79. Flute, oboe, clarinet
    and piano.

Tchaikovsky, Peter Ilyich (1840–1893)
*Festival Overture on the Danish National Hymn.* Opus 15. Orchestral work.


·DEVIL — see also Hell

Gluck, Christoph Willibald (1714–1787)
"Dance of the Furies" from *Orpheus and Eurydice.* Orchestral work.
Hadley, Henry (1871–1937)
*Lucifer.* Opus 66. Orchestral work.
Liszt, Franz (1811–1886)
*Mephisto Waltz.* Piano; orchestral work.
"Mephistopheles" from *Faust Symphony.* Orchestral work.
Loeffler, Charles Martin (1861–1935)
*La Villanelle du Diable* (The devil's villanelle). Opus 9. Orchestral work.
Moore, Douglas (1893–1969)
*The Devil and Daniel Webster.* Opera.
Mussorgsky, Modest (1839–1881)
*Night on Bald Mountain.* Orchestral work.
Schuller, Gunther (1925–
"Little Blue Devil" from *Seven Studies on Themes of Paul Klee.* Orchestral work.
Scriabin, Alexander (1872–1915)
*Satanique poème.* Opus 36. Piano.
Stravinsky, Igor (1882–1971)
"Devil's Dance" and "Triumphal March of the Devil" from *L'Histoire du soldat* (The soldier's tale). Narrator and ballet.
Tartini, Giuseppe (1692–1770)
Sonata in G minor *The Devil's Trill.* Violin.


DOGS — see also Animals

Carpenter, John Alden (1876–1951)
"The Dogs" from *Adventures in a Perambulator.* Orchestral work.
Villa–Lobos, Heitor (1887–1959)
"Rubber Dog" from *Os animalinhos* (Little toy animals) from *Prole do bêbê* (Baby's playthings) No. 2. Piano.

DOLLS — see also Children, Marionettes and Puppets

Bizet, Georges (1838–1875)
"La Poupée" (The doll) from *Jeux d'enfants* (Children's games).
Piano duet.
Debussy, Claude (1862–1918)
"General Lavine – eccentric" from *Préludes II*. Piano.
"Serenade for the Doll" from *Children's Corner*. Piano.
Delibes, Léo (1836–1891)
*Coppélia*. Ballet.
Elgar, Edward (1857–1934)
"The Serious Doll," "The Sad Doll" and "The Merry Doll" from
*Nursery Suite*. Opus 86. Orchestral work.
Fauré, Gabriel (1845–1924)
*Dolly Suite*. Opus 56. Piano duet. Six movements: (1) "Berceuse"
(Lullaby) (2) "Mi–a–ou" (3) "Le Jardin de Dolly" (Dolly's garden)
(4) "Kitty–Valse" (5) "Tendresse" (Tenderness) (6) "Le Pas
espagnol" (Spanish dance).
Villa–Lobos, Heitor (1887–1959)
*A familia do bêbê* (Dolls) from *Prole do bêbê* (Baby's playthings)
No. 1. Piano. Eight movements: (1) "Porcelain" (2) "Paper"
(3) "Clay" (4) "Rubber" (5) "Wooden" (6) "Rag" (7) "Punch"
(8) "Witch Doll."

DON JUAN — see also Love

Gluck, Christoph Willibald (1714–1787)
*Don Juan*. Ballet.
Mozart, Wolfgang Amadeus (1756–1791)
*Don Giovanni* (Don Juan). K. 527. Opera.
Strauss, Richard (1864–1949)
*Don Juan*. Opus 20. Orchestral work.
Szymanowski, Karol (1882–1937)
"Sérénade de Don Juan" from *Masques*. Opus 34. Piano.

DON QUIXOTE — see also Knights

Esplá, Oscar (1886–1976)
*Don Quixote velando las armas* (Don Quixote watching over his
arms). Orchestral work.
Gerhard, Roberto (1896–1970)
*Don Quixote*. Ballet.
Massenet, Jules (1842–1912)
*Don Quichotte*. Opera.

Purcell, Henry (1659–1695)
*Don Quixote.* Incidental music.
Rubinstein, Anton (1829–1894)
*Don Quixote.* Opus 87. Orchestral work.
Strauss, Richard (1864–1949)
*Don Quixote.* Opus 35. Orchestral work. Ten variations:
(1) "The Knight and his Squire Start on their Journey"
(2) "The Victorious Battle against the Host of the Great Emperor
Alifanfaron" (3) "Colloquies of Knight and Squire"
(4) "The Adventure with the Penitents" (5) "The Knight's Vigil"
(6) "The Meeting with Dulcinea" (7) "The Ride through the Air"
(8) "The Journey in the Enchanted Park" (9) "The Combat with
Two Magicians" (10) "The Knight of the White Moon"
(Finale) "The Death of Don Quixote."
Weinberger, Jaromir (1896–1967)
*Don Quixote.* Orchestral work.


DREAM — see also Sleep

Balakirev, Mily (1837–1910)
*Berceuse.* Piano.
Berlioz, Hector (1803–1869)
*Symphonie fantastique* (Fantastic symphony). Opus 14.
Five movements: (1) "Dreams, Passions" (2) "The Ball"
(3) "Scene in the Country" (4) "March to the Gallows" (5) "Dream
of the Witches' Sabbath."
Elgar, Edward (1857–1934)
*Dream Children.* Opus 43. Orchestral work.
Mendelssohn, Felix (1809–1847)
*A Midsummer Night's Dream.* Opus 21. Orchestral work.
Nielsen, Carl (1865–1931)
*Saga–Drøm* (A saga dream). Opus 39. Orchestral work.
Prokofiev, Sergei (1891–1953)
"Cinderella Dreams of the Ball" from *Cinderella.* Opus 87, No. 2.
Orchestral work.
Schumann, Robert (1810–1856)
"Träumerei" (Reverie) from *Kinderscenen* (Scenes from
childhood). Opus 15. Piano.
"Traumes Wirren" (Nightmares) from *Fantasiestücke* (Fantasy
pieces). Opus 12. Piano.
Strauss, Richard (1864–1949)
*Tod und Verklärung* (Death and transfiguration). Opus 24.
Orchestral work.
Tchaikovsky, Peter Ilyich (1840–1893)
Symphony No. 1 in G minor *Winter Daydreams.* Opus 13.

Wolf, Hugo (1860–1903)
"Penthesilea's Dream of the Feast of the Roses" from *Penthesilea.*
Orchestral work.


DWARFS — see also Fairy World

Grieg, Edvard (1843–1907)
"In the Hall of the Mountain King" from *Peer Gynt.* Suite 1.
Opus 46. Orchestral work.
"March of the Dwarfs" from *Lyric Suite.*
Opus 54. Piano.
Liszt, Franz (1811–1886)
"Gnomenreigen" (Dance of the gnomes) from *Two Concert Studies.*
Piano.
Mussorgsky, Modest (1839–1881)
"Gnomes" from *Pictures at an Exhibition.* Piano; orchestral work.
Ravel, Maurice (1875–1937)
"Scarbo" from *Gaspard de la nuit* (Scents of the night). Piano.


# E


EARTH — see also Countryside

Bloch, Ernest (1880–1959)
"1620. The Soil – the Indians – the Mayflower – the Landing
Pilgrims" from *America: An Epic Rhapsody.* Orchestral work.
Hadley, Henry (1871–1937)
Symphony No. 4 in D minor *North, East, South, West.* Opus 64.
Liszt, Franz (1811–1886)
"Paysage" (Landscape) from *Etudes d' exécution transcendante*
(Transcendental Etudes). Piano.
Stravinsky, Igor (1882–1971)
*Le Sacre du printemps* (The rite of spring). Ballet.
Part I: The Adoration of the Earth. Introduction – Harbingers of
Spring – Dance of the Adolescents – Spring Rounds – Games of
the Round Cities – The Procession of the Wise Men – The
Adoration of the Earth – Dance of the Earth.
Part II: The Sacrifice. Introduction – Mysterious Circle of the
Adolescents – Glorification of the Chosen One – Evocation of
the Ancestors – The Sacrificial Dance of the Chosen One.

EASTER — see also Bible, Christ, Christmas

Foerster, Josef Bohuslav (1859–1951)
    Symphony No. 4 in C minor *Easter Eve*. Opus 54.
Hanson, Howard (1896–1981)
    Symphony No. 5 *Sinfonia sacra*. Opus 43.
Mahler, Gustav (1860–1911)
    Symphony No. 2 in C minor *Resurrection*.
Rimsky–Korsakov, Nikolai (1844–1908)
    *Russian Easter Overture*. Opus 36. Orchestral work.
Turina, Joaquín (1882–1949)
    "Le Jeudi saint à minuit" (Holy Thursday at midnight) from
        *Seville*. Opus 2. Piano.
Wagner, Richard (1813–1883)
    "Prelude and Good Friday Music" from *Parsifal*. Orchestral work.


EGYPT

Chadwick, George (1854–1931)
    *Cleopatra*. Orchestral work.
Debussy, Claude (1862–1918)
    "Canope" (Canopic vase) from *Préludes II*. Piano.
    "Pour l'égyptienne" (For the Egyptian woman) from *Six Epigraphes
        antiques* (Six ancient inscriptions). Piano duet.
Ketelbey, Albert (1875–1959)
    *In the Mystic Land of Egypt*. Orchestral work.
Luigini, Alexandre (1850–1906)
    *Ballet égyptien*. Orchestral work.
Mozart, Wolfgang Amadeus (1756–1791)
    *Thamos, König in Aegypten* (Thamos, King of Egypt). K. 345.
        Incidental music.
Prokofiev, Sergei (1891–1953)
    *Egyptian Night*. Opus 61. Orchestral work.
Strauss, Johann Jr. (1825–1899)
    *Egyptischer Marsch* (Egyptian march). Opus 335. Orchestral work.
Strauss, Richard (1864–1949)
    *Die Ägyptische Helena* (The Egyptian Helen). Opera.
Verdi, Giuseppe (1813–1901)
    *Aida*. Opera.


ELEPHANTS — see also Animals

Debussy, Claude (1862–1918)
    "Jimbo's Lullaby" from *Children's Corner*. Piano.

Poulenc, Francis (1899–1963)
*L'Histoire de Babar le petit éléphant* (The story of Babar the little elephant). Narrator and orchestra.
Saint-Saëns, Camille (1835–1921)
"Elephants" from *Le Carnaval des animaux: fantaisie zoologique* (Carnival of the animals). Orchestral work.
Stravinsky, Igor (1882–1971)
*Polka for Circus Elephants.* Orchestral work.


ENGLAND — see also Cities (London)

Bach, Johann Sebastian (1685–1750)
*English Suites* (6). Harpischord.
Bax, Arnold (1883–1953)
*Tintagel.* Orchestral work.
Vaughan Williams, Ralph (1872–1958)
*English Folk Song Suite.* Military band. Three movements:
(1) "Seventeen Come Sunday" (2) "Folksongs from Somerset" (3) "My Bonnie Boy."
Norfolk Rhapsody No. 1 in E minor. Orchestral work.


EVENING — see also Afternoon, Day, Morning, Night, Noon, Sunrise, Sunset

Falla, Manuel de (1876–1946)
"Gypsies – Evening" from *El Amor brujo* (Love, the magician). Ballet.
Grieg, Edvard (1843–1907)
*Evening in the Mountains.* Opus 68. Orchestral work.
Griffes, Charles Tomlinson (1884–1920)
*The Lake at Evening.* Orchestral work.
Haydn, Franz Joseph (1732–1809)
Symphony No. 8 in G major *Le Soir* (Evening).
Kodály, Zoltán (1882–1967)
*Nyári este* (Summer evening). Orchestral work.
Liszt, Franz (1811–1886)
"Harmonies du soir" (Evening harmonies) from *Etudes d'exécution transcendante* (Transcendental Etudes). Piano.
Piston, Walter (1894–1976)
"Summer Evening" from *Three New England Sketches.* Orchestral work.
Prokofiev, Sergei (1891–1953)
"Evening" from *Summer Day.* Opus 65a. Orchestral work.
Schumann, Robert (1810–1856)
"Des Abends" (At evening) from *Fantasiestücke.* Opus 12. Piano.

Siegmeister, Elie (1909–
"Harvest Evening" from *Prairie Legend.* Orchestral work.

# F

FAIRY TALES — see also Folk Tales, Greek Myths, Literature, Tales

Davies, Henry Walford (1869–1941)
*Peter Pan.* Opus 30. String quartet.
Delius, Frederick (1862–1934)
*Eventyr (Once upon a time).* Orchestral work.
Dvořák, Antonín (1841–1904)
*The Golden Spinning–Wheel.* Opus 109. Orchestral work.
*The Noonday Witch.* Opus 108. Orchestral work.
*The Water–Goblin.* Opus 107. Orchestral work.
*The Wild Dove.* Opus 110. Orchestral work.
Humperdinck, Engelbert (1854–1921)
*Hansel und Gretel.* Opera.
Janáček, Leos (1854–1928)
*Fairy Tale.* Cello and piano.
Liadov, Anatol (1855–1914)
*Baba Yaga.* Opus 56. Orchestral work.
*Kikimora.* Opus 63. Orchestral work.
*The Enchanted Lake.* Opus 62. Orchestral work.
MacDowell, Edward (1860–1908)
*Forgotten Fairy Tales.* Opus 4. Piano. Four movements:
(1) "Sung outside the Prince's Door" (2) "Of a Tailor and a Bear"
(3) "Beauty in the Rose–Garden" (4) "From Dwarfland."
*Moon Pictures.* Opus 21. Piano duet. Five movements:
(1) "The Hindoo Maiden" (2) "Stork's Story" (3) "In Tyrol"
(4) "The Swan" (5) "Visit of the Bear." (Inspired by Hans
Christian Andersen.)
Massenet, Jules (1842–1912)
*Cendrillon* (Cinderella). Opera.
Medtner, Nikolai (1880–1951)
*Fairy Tales.* Opuses 8, 9, 14, 20, 26, 34, 35, 42, 51. Piano.
Sonata No. 1 in C minor *Fairy Tale.* Opus 25. Piano.
*Two Fairy Tales.* Opus 48. Piano. Two movements:
(1) "Dance Fairy Tale" (2) "Elf Fairy Tale."
Prokofiev, Sergei (1891–1953)
*Cinderella.* Opus 87. Two ballet suites.
Suite No. 1: (1) "Introduction" (2) "Pas de Chat" (3) "Quarrel"
(4) "Fairy Godmother and Fairy Winter" (5) "Mazurka"
(6) "Cinderella Goes to the Ball" (7) "Cinderella's Waltz" and
"Midnight."

Suite No. 2: (1) "Cinderella Dreams of the Ball" (2) "Dancing
Lessons and Gavotte" (3) "Fairy Spring and Fairy Summer"
(4) "Bourrée" (5) "Cinderella and the Castle" (6) "Galop."
*Peter and the Wolf.* Opus 67. Narrator and orchestra.
*The Love of Three Oranges.* Opus 33. Opera.
*The Ugly Duckling.* Opus 18. Orchestral work.
Rachmaninoff, Sergei (1873–1943)
"Little Red Riding Hood" from *Etudes–Tableaux.* Opus 39, No. 6.
Piano.
Ravel, Maurice (1875–1937)
*Ma Mère l' Oye* (Mother Goose suite). Orchestral work; piano duet.
Five movements: (1) "Pavane de la belle au bois dormant" (Pavane
of Sleeping Beauty) (2) "Petit Poucet" (Tom Thumb)
(3) "Laideronette, impératrice des pagodas" (Little ugly one,
empress of the pagodas) (4) "Les Entretiens de la belle et la bête"
(Conversations with beauty and the beast) (5) "Le Jardin féerique"
(The fairy garden).
Schumann, Robert (1810–1856)
*Märchener zählungen* (Fairytales). Opus 132. Clarinet, viola and
piano.
Stravinsky, Igor (1882–1971)
*Le Chant du rossignol* (The nightingale's song). Ballet;
orchestral work. Three movements: (1) "The Palace of the
Chinese Emperor" (2) "The Two Nightingales" (3) "Illness
and Recovery of the Chinese Emperor."
*L'Oiseau de feu* (The firebird). Ballet.
*Le Rossignol* (The nightingale). Opera.
Tchaikovsky, Peter Ilyich (1840–1893)
*La Belle au bois dormant* (Sleeping beauty). Opus 66. Ballet.
Toch, Ernst (1887–1964)
*Peter Pan.* Opus 76. Orchestral work.
*Pinocchio.* Orchestral work.
Zádor, Eugene (1894–1977)
"Fairy Tale" from *Children's Symphony.* Orchestral work.


FAIRY WORLD — see also Dwarfs, Sirens, Spirits,
Will–o'–the–Wisp

Bax, Arnold (1883–1953)
*In the Faëry Hills.* Orchestral work.
*Nympholept.* Orchestral work.
Berlioz, Hector (1803–1869)
"Dance of the Sylphs" from *La Damnation de Faust* (The damnation
of Faust). Opus 24. Orchestral work.
Berwald, Franz (1796–1868)
*Elfenspiel* (Elves' games). Orchestral work.

Chopin, Frederic (1810–1849)
  Ballade No. 3 in A–flat major. Opus 47. Piano.
Debussy, Claude (1862–1918)
  "La Danse de Puck" from *Préludes I*. Piano.
  "Les Fées sont d'exquises danseuses" (Fairies are exquisite dancers)
    and "Ondine" from *Préludes II*. Piano.
Delius, Frederick (1862–1934)
  *Eventyr (Once upon a time)*. Orchestral work.
Dvořák, Antonín (1841–1904)
  *The Water–Goblin*. Opus 107. Orchestral work.
Elgar, Edward (1857–1934)
  "Fairies and Giants" and "Fairy Pipers" from *Wand of Youth Suite
    No. 2*. Opus 1a. Orchestral work.
Goldmark, Carl (1830–1915)
  *Sakuntala*. Opus 13. Orchestral work.
Grieg, Edvard (1843–1907)
  "Puck" from *Lyric Pieces*. Opus 71, No. 3. Piano.
Medtner, Nikolai (1880–1951)
  "Elf Fairy Tale" from *Two Fairy Tales*. Opus 48. Piano.
Mendelssohn, Felix (1809–1847)
  *A Midsummer Night's Dream*. Opus 21. Orchestral work.
  *Die Schöne Melusine* (The beautiful Melusina). Opus 32.
    Orchestral work.
Prokofiev, Sergei (1891–1953)
  "Fairy Godmother and Fairy Winter" from *Cinderella*. Suite No. 1.
    Opus 87. Orchestral work.
  "Fairy Spring and Fairy Summer" from *Cinderella*. Suite No. 2.
    Opus 87. Orchestral work.
Purcell, Henry (1659–1695)
  *The Fairy Queen*. Opera.
Ravel, Maurice (1875–1937)
  "Le Jardin féerique" (The fairy garden) from *Ma Mère l'Oye* (Mother
    Goose suite). Orchestral work; piano duet.
  "Ondine" from *Gaspard de la nuit* (Scents of the night). Piano.
Stravinsky, Igor (1882–1971)
  *Le Baiser de la fée* (The fairy's kiss). Ballet.
Tchaikovsky, Peter Ilyich (1840–1893)
  "Dance of the Sugarplum Fairy" from *The Nutcracker*. Opus 71a.
    Ballet.
  "Lilac Fairy" from *La Belle au bois dormant* (Sleeping beauty).
    Opus 66. Ballet.
Weber, Carl Maria von (1786–1826)
  *Oberon*. Opera.

# FAMILY

Bach, Johann Sebastian (1685–1750)
*Capriccio sopra la lontananza del suo fratella dilettissimo* (On the departure of his beloved brother). Piano, harpischord.
Bizet, Georges (1838–1875)
"Petit mari, petite femme" (Little husband, little wife) from *Jeux d'enfants* (Children's games). Piano duet.
Busoni, Ferruccio (1866–1924)
*Berceuse élégiaque*. Opus 42. Orchestral work.
Copland, Aaron (1900–
"Grandfather's Story" from *The Red Pony*. Orchestral work.
Piston, Walter (1894–1976)
"Tango of The Four Daughters" from *The Incredible Flutist*. Ballet.
Prokofiev, Sergei (1891–1953)
Grandfather motif from *Peter and the Wolf*. Opus 67.
Narrator and orchestra.
Sibelius, Jean (1865–1957)
"The Three Blind Sisters" from *Pelléas et Mélisande*. Opus 46.
Orchestral work.
Thomson, Virgil (1896–
*Family Portrait*. Brass quintet.


# FARM and FARMERS

Copland, Aaron (1900–
*The Tender Land*. Opera.
Khachaturian, Aram (1903–1978)
*Gayane*. Ballet.
Moore, Douglas (1893–1969)
*Farm Journal*. Chamber orchestra. Four movements:
(1) "Up Early" (2) "Sunday Clothes" (3) "Lamplight"
(4) "Harvest Song."
Schumann, Robert (1810–1856)
"Fröhlicher Landmann" (Happy farmer) from *Album für die Jugend* (Album for the young). Opus 68. Piano.
Thomson, Virgil (1896–
*The Plow that Broke the Plains*. Orchestral work.
Six movements: (1) "Prelude" (2) "Pastorale" (Grass) (3) "Cattle"
(4) "Blues" (Speculation) (5) "Drought" (6) "Devastation."
*Wheat Field at Noon*. Orchestral work.
Zádor, Eugene (1894–1977)
"The Farm" from *Children's Symphony*.

# FATE

Beethoven, Ludwig van (1770–1827)
 Symphony No. 5 in C minor. Opus 67.
Mahler, Gustav (1860–1911)
 Symphony No. 9 in D minor.
Tchaikovsky, Peter Ilyich (1840–1893)
 Symphony No. 5 in E minor. Opus 64.

# FAUST — see also Devil

Berlioz, Hector (1803–1869)
 *La Damnation de Faust* (The damnation of Faust). Opus 24.
  Opera; orchestral work.
Boïto, Arrigo (1842–1918)
 *Mefistofele*. Opera.
Busoni, Ferruccio (1866–1924)
 *Doktor Faust*. Opus 51. Opera; orchestral work.
Gounod, Charles (1818–1893)
 *Faust*. Opera.
Liszt, Franz (1811–1886)
 *Faust*. Orchestral work.
 *Faust Symphony*. Three movements: (1) "Faust" (2) "Marguerite"
  (3) "Mephistopheles."
 *Mephisto Waltz*. Orchestral work.
Rabaud, Henri (1873–1949)
 *La Procession nocturne* (Nocturnal procession). Orchestral work.
Rubinstein, Anton (1829–1894)
 *Faust*. Opus 68. Orchestral work.
Wagner, Richard (1813–1883)
 *Eine Faust Ouvertüre*. Orchestral work.

# FESTIVALS — see also Carnivals

Beethoven, Ludwig van (1770–1827)
 "Village Festival" from Symphony No. 6 in F major *Pastorale*.
  Opus 68.
Chausson, Ernest (1855–1899)
 *Soir de fête* (Festival evening). Opus 32. Orchestral work.
Debussy, Claude (1862–1918)
 "Le Matin d'un jour de fête" (Morning of a festival day) from *Iberia*.
  Orchestral work.
Harty, Herbert Hamilton (1879–1941)
 "The Fair Day" from *Irish Symphony*.

Ibert, Jacques (1890–1962)
"The Fair" from *Paris*. Orchestral work.
Ravel, Maurice (1875–1937)
"Feria" (Fair) from *Rapsodie espagnole* (Spanish rhapsody).
Orchestral work.
Respighi, Ottorino (1879–1936)
*Feste romane* (Roman festivals). Orchestral work.
Rimsky–Korsakov, Nikolai (1844–1908)
"The Festival at Bagdad" from *Scheherazade*. Opus 35.
Orchestral work.
Schuman, William (1910–
*American Festival Overture*. Orchestral work.
Shostakovich, Dmitri (1906–1975)
*Festival Overture*. Opus 96. Orchestral work.
Siegmeister, Elie (1909–
"Country Fair" from *Prairie Legend*. Orchestral work.


# FINLAND

Glazunov, Alexander (1865–1936)
*A Karelian Legend*. Opus 98. Orchestral work.
*Finnish Fantasy*. Opus 88. Orchestral work.
*Finnish Sketches*. Opus 89. Orchestral work. Two movements:
(1) "From the 'Kalevala'" (2) "Cortege."
Kajanus, Robert (1856–1933)
*Two Finnish Rhapsodies*. Orchestral work.
Klami, Uuno (1900–1961)
*Helsinki March*. Opus 22. Orchestral work.
*Kalevala Suite*. Opus 23. Orchestral work.
*Karelian Rhapsody*. Opus 15. Orchestral work.
*Lemminkäinen*. Opus 24. Orchestral work.
Madetoja, Leevi (1887–1947)
*Kullervo*. Opus 15. Orchestral work.
Palmgren, Selim (1878–1951)
*Finnish Lyric Pieces*. Piano.
*From Finland*. Orchestral work.
Sibelius, Jean (1865–1957)
*En Saga*. Opus 9. Orchestral work.
*Finlandia*. Opus 26. Orchestral work.
*Four Legends*. Opus 22. Orchestral work. Four movements:
(1) "Lemminkäinen and the Maidens" (2) "Lemminkäinen in
Tuonela" (3) "The Swan of Tuonela" (4) "Lemminkäinen's
Homeward Journey."
*Karelia Suite*. Opus 11. Orchestral work.
*Pohjola's Daughter*. Opus 49. Orchestral work.
*Scènes historiques*. Opus 25. Orchestral work.
*Tapiola*. Opus 112. Orchestral work.

# FIRE and FIREWORKS

Bax, Arnold (1883–1953)
 *Spring Fire*. Orchestral work.
Debussy, Claude (1862–1918)
 "Feu d'artifice" (Fireworks) from *Préludes II*. Piano.
Falla, Manuel de (1876–1946)
 "Ritual Fire Dance" from *El Amor brujo* (Love, the magician). Ballet.
Handel, George Frideric (1685–1759)
 *Royal Fireworks Music*. Orchestral work.
Haydn, Franz Joseph (1732–1809)
 Symphony No. 59 in A major *Feuersymphonie* (Fire symphony).
MacDowell, Edward (1860–1908)
 *Fireside Tales*. Opus 61. Piano. Six movements:
  (1) "An Old Love Story" (2) "Of Brer Rabbit" (3) "From a German Forest" (4) "Of Salamanders" (5) "A Haunted House" (6) "By Smoldering Embers."
Satie, Erik (1866–1925)
 "Feu d'artifice" (Fireworks) from *Sports et divertissements* (Sports and entertainments). Piano.
Schumann, Robert (1810–1856)
 "Am Kamin" (At the fireside) from *Kinderzenen* (Scenes from childhood). Opus 15. Piano
Scriabin, Alexander (1872–1915)
 *Vers la flamme* (Toward the flame). Opus 72. Piano.
 *Prometheus: Poem of Fire*. Opus 60. Orchestral work.
Stravinsky, Igor (1882–1971)
 *Feu d'artifice* (Fireworks). Opus 4. Orchestral work.
 *L'Oiseau de feu* (The firebird). Ballet.
Wagner, Richard (1813–1883)
 "Magic Fire Music" from *Die Walküre*. Orchestral work.


# FISH — see also Animals

Debussy, Claude (1862–1918)
 "Poissons d'or" (Goldfish) from *Images II*. Piano.
Saint–Saëns, Camille (1835–1921)
 "Aquarium" from *Le Carnaval des animaux: fantaisie zoologique* (Carnival of the animals). Orchestral work.
Schubert, Franz (1797–1828)
 Quintet in A major *Forellenquintet* (Trout quintet). Opus 114. Piano quintet.

FLOWERS — see also Garden

Castelnuovo–Tedesco, Mario (1895–1968)
   "Minuet of the Rose" from *The Birthday of the Infanta*. Orchestral
   work.
Glière, Reinhold (1875–1956)
   *The Red Poppy*. Opus 70. Ballet.
MacDowell, Edward (1860–1908)
   "The Bluebell" from *Six Idyls after Goethe*. Opus 28. Piano.
   "To a Water Lily" and "To a Wild Rose" from *Woodland Sketches*.
   Opus 51. Piano.
   "With Sweet Lavender" from *New England Idyls*. Opus 62. Piano.
Ravel, Maurice (1875–1937)
   *Adélaïde, ou le langage des fleurs* (Adelaide, or the language of
   flowers). Ballet.
Schumann, Robert (1810–1856)
   *Blumenstück* (Flower piece). Opus 19. Piano.
   "Einsame Blumen" (Lonely flower) from *Waldscenen* (Forest scenes).
   Opus 82. Piano.
Scott, Cyril (1879–1970)
   *Asphodel*. Piano.
Strauss, Johann Jr. (1825–1899)
   *Myrthenblüten* (Myrtle blossom). Opus 395. Waltz.
   *Rosen aus dem Süden* (Roses from the south). Opus 388. Waltz.
Strauss, Richard (1864–1949)
   *Der Rosenkavalier* (The knight of the rose). Opus 59. Opera.
Taylor, Deems (1885–1966)
   "Dedication: The Garden of Live Flowers" from *Through the Looking
   Glass*. Orchestral work.
Tchaikovsky, Peter Ilyich (1840–1893)
   "Waltz of the Flowers" from *The Nutcracker*. Opus 71. Ballet.
Villa–Lobos, Heitor (1887–1959)
   *Distribução de flores* (Distributions of flowers). Flute and guitar.
Wagner, Richard (1813–1883)
   "Flower Maidens' Scene" from *Parsifal*. Orchestral work.


FOLK TALES — see also Fairy Tales, Greek Myths, Literature, Tales

Casella, Alfredo (1883–1947)
   *La Giara* (The jug). Ballet.
Copland, Aaron (1900–
   *Billy the Kid*. Ballet.

Glière, Reinhold (1875–1956)
  Symphony No. 3 in B minor *Ilia Mourometz*. Opus 42.
    Four movements: (1) "Wandering Pilgrims: Ilia Mourometz and
    Sviatogar" (2) "Solovei the Brigand" (3) "The Palace of Prince
    Vladimir" (4) "The Feats of Valor and the Petrification of Ilia
    Mourometz."
Indy, Vincent d' (1851–1931)
  *Istar*. Opus 42. Orchestral work.
Kodály, Zoltán (1882–1967)
  *Háry János*. Orchestral work. Six movements:
    (1) "Prelude: The Fairy Story Begins" (2) "The Viennese Musical
    Clock" (3) "Song" (4) "The Battle and Defeat of Napoleon"
    (5) "Intermezzo" (6) "Entrance of the Emperor and his Court."
Mendelssohn, Felix (1809–1847)
  *Die Schöne Melusine* (The beautiful Melusina).
    Opus 32. Orchestral work.
Rimsky–Korsakov, Nikolai (1844–1908)
  Symphony No. 2 *Antar*. Opus 9.
Rossini, Gioacchino (1792–1868)
  *Guillaume Tell* (William Tell). Opera.
Sibelius, Jean (1865–1957)
  *Karelia Suite*. Opus 11. Orchestral work.
  *Pohjola's Daughter*. Opus 49. Orchestral work.
Strauss, Richard (1864–1949)
  *Till Eulenspiegels lustige Streiche* (Till Eulenspiegel's merry
    pranks). Opus 28. Orchestral work.
Stravinsky, Igor (1882–1971)
  *L'Oiseau de feu* (The firebird). Ballet.
Weber, Carl Maria von (1786–1826)
  *Der Freischütz* (The free shooter). Opera.
Weinberger, Jaromir (1896–1967)
  *Swanda der Dudelsackpfeifer* (Swanda, the bagpipe player). Opera.


## FOOD and DRINK

Milhaud, Darius (1892–1974)
  *Le Bœuf sur le toit* (The nothing–doing bar). Opus 58. Ballet.
Prokofiev, Sergei (1891–1953)
  *The Love of Three Oranges*. Opus 33. Opera.
Saint–Saëns, Camille (1835–1921)
  *Wedding–Cake*. Opus 76. Strings and piano.
Satie, Erik (1866–1925)
  *Trois morceaux en forme de poire* (Three pieces in the shape of a
    pear). Piano duet.
Strauss, Johann Jr. (1825–1899)
  *Wein, Weib und Gesang* (Wine, women and song). Opus 333. Waltz.
  *Wiener Bonbons* (Vienna bonbons). Opus 307. Waltz.

Strauss, Richard (1864–1949)
"The Dinner" from *Le Bourgeois gentilhomme*. Opus 66. Orchestral work.
Tchaikovsky, Peter Ilyich (1840–1893)
*Nutcracker Suite*. Opus 71a. Ballet. Eight movements:
(1) "Overture" (2) "March" (3) "Dance of the Sugarplum Fairy" (4) "Russian Dance" (5) "Arabian Dance" (6) "Chinese Dance" (7) "Dance of the Flutes" (8) "Waltz of the Flowers."
Telemann, George Philipp (1681–1767)
*Musique de table* (Table music). Chamber music.

FOREST — see also Leaves, Trees

Bauer, Marion (1897–1955)
*From New Hampshire Woods*. Opus 12. Piano.
Bax, Arnold (1883–1953)
*November Woods*. Orchestral work.
*The Happy Forest*. Orchestral work.
*The Tale the Pine Trees Knew*. Orchestral work.
Byrd, William (1543–1623)
"Will you Walk the Woods so Wild" from *My Ladye Nevells Booke*. Harpsichord.
Debussy, Claude (1862–1918)
"Cloches à travers les feuilles" (Bells through the leaves) from *Images II*. Piano.
Dvořák, Antonín (1841–1904)
*From the Bohemian Forest*. Opus 68. Piano duet. Six movements:
(1) "In the Spinning–Room" (2) "On the Dark Lake" (3) "Witches' Sabbath" (4) "On the Watch" (5) "Silent Woods" (6) "In Troubled Times."
*Silent Woods*. Opus 68. Cello and orchestra.
Glazunov, Alexander (1865–1936)
*The Forest*. Opus 19. Orchestral work.
Indy, Vincent d' (1851–1931)
*La Forêt enchantée* (The enchanted forest). Opus 8. Orchestral work.
Liszt, Franz (1811–1886)
"Waldesrauschen" (Forest murmurs) from *Two Concert Studies*. Piano.
MacDowell, Edward (1860–1908)
*Forest Idyls*. Opus 19. Piano. Four movements:
(1) "Forest Stillness" (2) "Play of the Nymphs" (3) "Revery" (4) "Dance of the Dryads."
"In Deep Woods" from *New England Idyls*. Opus 62. Piano.

"Woodland Sketches." Opus 51. Piano. Ten movements:
(1) "To a Wild Rose" (2) "Will–o'–the–Wisp" (3) "At an Old
Trysting Place" (4) "In Autumn" (5) "From an Indian Lodge"
(6) "To a Water–Lily" (7) "From Uncle Remus" (8) "A Deserted
Farm" (9) "By a Meadow Brook" (10) "Told at Sunset."
Schumann, Robert (1810–1856)
*Waldscenen* (Forest scenes). Opus 82. Piano. Nine movements:
(1) "Eintritt" (Entrance) (2) "Jäger auf der Lauer" (Hunter in wait)
(3) "Einsame Blumen" (Lonely flower) (4) "Verrufene Stelle"
(Ill–reputed spot) (5) "Freundliche Landschaft" (Friendly
Countryside) (6) "Herberge" (Shelter) (7) "Vogel als Prophet"
(Bird as prophet) (8) "Jagdlied" (Hunting song) (9) "Abschied"
(Departure).
Sibelius, Jean (1865–1957)
*Tapiola.* Opus 112. Orchestral work.
Strauss, Johann Jr. (1825–1899)
*Geschichten aus dem Wienerwald* (Tales from the Vienna woods).
Opus 325. Waltz.
Villa–Lobos, Heitor (1887–1959)
*Dawn in a Tropical Forest.* Orchestral work.
"Woodland Memory" from *Bachianas brasileiras.* No. 2. Orchestral
work.
Wagner, Richard (1813–1883)
"Waldweben" (Forest murmurs) from *Siegfried.* Orchestral work.


FOUNTAIN — see also Water

Elgar, Edward (1857–1934)
"Fountain Dance" from *Wand of Youth Suite* No. 2. Opus 1b.
Orchestral work.
Griffes, Charles Tomlinson (1884–1920)
"The Fountain at Acqua Paola" from *Four Roman Sketches.* Opus 7.
Piano; orchestral work.
Liszt, Franz (1811–1886)
"Les Jeux d'eau à la Villa d'Este" (The fountains at the Villa
d'Este) from *Années de pèlerinage: Troisième année* (Years of
pilgrimage: third year). Piano.
Prokofiev, Sergei (1891–1953)
"Romeo at the Fountain" from *Romeo and Juliet.* Opus 64–bis.
Orchestral work.
Ravel, Maurice (1875–1937)
*Jeux d'eau* (The fountain). Piano.

Respighi, Ottorino (1879–1936)
   *Fontane di Roma* (Fountains of Rome). Orchestral work.
   Four movements: (1) "La Fontana di Valle Giulia all' alba" (The
   fountain of Valle Giulia at dawn) (2) "La Fontana del Tritone al
   mattino" (The fountain at Triton in the morning) (3) "La Fontana di
   Trevi al meriggio" (The fountain of Trevi at midday)
   (4) "La Fontana di Villa Medici al tramonto" (The fountain of the
   Villa Medici at dusk).
Sibelius, Jean (1865–1957)
   "A Fountain in the Park" from *Pelléas et Mélisande*. Opus 46.
   Orchestral work.


FRANCE — see also Cities (Paris)

Bach, Johann Sebastian (1685–1750)
   *French Suites* (6). Piano, harpsichord.
Bizet, Georges (1838–1875)
   *L'Arlésienne* (A woman of Arles). Orchestral work.
Haydn, Franz Joseph (1732–1809)
   Symphony No. 85 in B–flat major *La Reine* (The queen).
Indy, Vincent d' (1851–1931)
   *Symphonie sur un chant montagnard français* (Symphony on a
   French mountain song). Opus 25. Piano and orchestra.
Kodály, Zoltán (1882–1967)
   "The Battle and Defeat of Napoleon" from *Háry János*. Orchestral
   work.
Massenet, Jules (1842–1912)
   *Scènes alsaciennes*. Orchestral work.
Milhaud, Darius (1892–1974)
   *Suite française*. Orchestral work. Five movements:
   (1) "Normandie" (2) "Bretagne" (3) "Ile–de–France"
   (4) "Alsace–Lorraine" (5) "Provence."
   *Suite provençale*. Orchestral work.
   Symphony No. 4 *1848*. Opus 281. Four movements:
   (1) "Insurrection" (2) "To the Dead of the Republic"
   (3) "The Peaceful Joys of Liberty Regained"
   (4) "Commemoration, 1948."


FUNERAL — see also Death

Beethoven, Ludwig van (1770–1827)
   Sonata No. 12 in A–flat major, Movement 3. Opus 26. Piano.
   Symphony No. 3 in E–flat major *Eroica,* Movement 2. Opus 55.

Bloch, Ernest (1880–1959)
  "Cortège funèbre" (Funeral procession) from *Trois poèmes juifs*
  (Three Jewish poems). Orchestral work.
Chopin, Frederic (1810–1849)
  "Marche funèbre" (Funeral march) from Sonata No. 2 in B–flat minor.
  Opus 35. Piano.
Glazunov, Alexander (1865–1936)
  "Cortege" from *Finnish Sketches*. Opus 89. Orchestral work.
Gounod, Charles (1818–1893)
  *Funeral March of a Marionette.* Orchestral work.
Liszt, Franz (1811–1886)
  "Funérailles" from *Harmonies poétiques et religieuses* (Religious and
  poetic harmonies). Piano.
  "Marche funèbre" (Funeral march) from *Années de pèlerinage:
  Troisième année* (Years of pilgrimage: third year). Piano.
Lutoslawski, Witold (1913–
  *Musique funèbre* (Funeral music). String orchestra.
Malipiero, Gian Francesco (1882–1973)
  "Funeral March" from *Pause del silenzio* (Silent pause). Orchestral
  work.
Mendelssohn, Felix (1809–1847)
  "Trauermarsch" (Funeral march) from *Lieder ohne Worte*
  (Songs without words). Opus 62, No. 3. Piano.
Prokofiev, Sergei (1891–1953)
  "Burial of Kije" from *Lieutenant Kije.* Opus 60. Orchestral work.
Wagner, Richard (1813–1883)
  "Siegfried's Funeral Music" from *Götterdämmerung* (Twilight of
  the Gods). Orchestral work.

# G

## GALLOWS

Berlioz, Hector (1803–1869)
  "March to the Gallows" from *Symphonie fantastique* (Fantastic
  symphony). Opus 14.
Ravel, Maurice (1875–1937)"Le Gibet" (The gallows) from *Gaspard de la
  nuit* (Scents of the night). Piano.

## GAMES — see also Sports

Bizet, Georges (1838–1875)
*Jeux d'enfants* (Games of children). Piano duet. Twelve movements: (1) "L'Escarpolette" (The swing) (2) "La Toupie" (The top) (3) "La Poupée" (The doll) (4) "Les Chevaux de bois" (Wooden horses) (5) "Le Volant" (Battledore and Shuttlecock) (6) "Trompette et tambour" (Trumpet and drum) (7) "Les Bulles de savon" (Soap bubbles) (8) "Les Quatre coins" (Puss in the corner) (9) "Colin–maillard" (Blind–man's bluff) (10) "Saute–mouton" (Leap–frog) (11) "Petit mari, petite femme" (Little husband, little wife) (12) "Le Bal" (The ball).

Bliss, Arthur (1891–1975)
*Checkmate.* Ballet. Six movements: (1) "Dance of the Four Knights" (2) "Entry of the Black Queen" (3) "The Red Knight" (4) "Ceremony of the Red Bishops" (5) "Death of the Red Knight" (6) "Finale – Checkmate."

Carpenter, John Alden (1876–1951)
"Games" from *The Birthday of the Infanta.* Orchestral work.

Copland, Aaron (1900–
"Card Game at Night" from *Billy the Kid.* Ballet.

Debussy, Claude (1862–1918)
*Les Jeux* (Games). Ballet.

Stravinsky, Igor (1882–1971)
*Jeu de cartes* (The card party). Ballet in "three deals." Three movements: (1) "Introduction, Pas d'Action, Dance of the Joker, Little Waltz" (2) "Introduction, March, Variation of the Four Queens, Variation of the Jack of Hearts, Coda, March and Ensemble" (3) "Introduction, Waltz–Minuet, Presto (Combat Between Spades and Hearts), Final Dance (Triumph of the Hearts).

## GARDEN — see also Flowers

Balakirev, Mily (1837–1910)
*Au Jardin* (In the garden). Piano.

Bax, Arnold (1883–1953)
*The Garden of Fand.* Orchestral work.

Byrd, William (1543–1623)
"All in the Garden Green" from *My Ladye Nevells Booke.* Piano, harpsichord.

Chasins, Abram (1903–
"Flirtation in a Chinese Garden" from *Three Chinese Pieces.* Orchestral work.

Debussy, Claude (1862–1918)
"Jardins sous la pluie" (Gardens in the rain) from *Estampes* (Engravings). Piano.

Delius, Frederick (1862–1934)
  "A Walk to the Paradise Garden" from *A Village Romeo and Juliet*.
  Orchestral work.
  *In a Summer Garden*. Orchestral work.
Falla, Manuel de (1876–1946)
  *Noches en los jardines de España* (Nights in the gardens of Spain).
  Three movements: (1) "En el Generalife" (At the Generalife)
  (2) "Danza Lejana" (A far–off dance) (3) "En los jardines de la
  Sierra de Córdoba" (In the gardens of the Sierra of Cordoba).
Goldmark, Carl (1830–1915)
  "In the Garden" from *Ländliche Hochzeit* (Rustic wedding
  symphony). Opus 26. Orchestral work.
Hovhaness, Alan (1911–
  *Koke no niwa* (Moss garden). Opus 181. Chamber music.
Ketelbey, Albert (1875–1959)
  *In a Chinese Temple Garden*. Orchestral work.
  *In a Monastery Garden*. Orchestral work.
Madetoja, Leevi (1887–1947)
  *Kuoleman puutarha* (The garden of death). Opus 41. Piano.
Martinu, Bohuslav (1890–1959)
  "The Parable of a Garden" from *Parables*. Orchestral work.
Ravel, Maurice (1875–1937)
  "Le Jardin féerique" (The fairy garden) from *Ma Mère l' Oye*
  (Mother Goose suite). Piano duet.
Respighi, Ottorino (1879–1936)
  "Butantan" (In a snake garden near Sao Paulo) from *Impressioni
  brasiliane* (Brazilian impressions). Orchestral work.
Sorabji, Kaikhosru Shapurji (1892–
  *Le Jardin parfumé* (The scented garden). Piano.
Taylor, Deems (1885–1966)
  "Dedication: The Garden of Live Flowers" from *Through the Looking
  Glass*. Orchestral work.


# GERMANY

Beethoven, Ludwig van (1770–1827)
  *Deutsche Tänze* (German dances) (12). Opus 140. Orchestral work.
Mozart, Wolfgang Amadeus (1756–1791)
  *Deutsche Tänze* (German dances). Köchel Nos. 509, 536, 567, 571,
  586, 600, 602, 605. Orchestral work.
Schubert, Franz (1797–1828)
  *Deutsche Tänze* (German dances) (54). Piano.
Schumann, Robert (1810–1856)
  Symphony No. 3 in E–flat major *Rhenish*. Opus 97.

## GHOSTS — see Spirits

## GNOMES — see Dwarfs

## GOODBYE

Bach, Johann Sebastian (1685–1750)
 *Capriccio sopra la lontananza del suo fratella dilettissimo*
 (On the departure of his beloved brother). Piano, harpischord.
Beethoven, Ludwig van (1770–1827)
 Sonata No. 26 in E–flat major *Les Adieux*. Opus 81a.
Haydn, Franz Joseph (1732–1809)
 Symphony No. 45 in F–sharp minor *Abschied Symphonie* (Farewell
 symphony).
Hovhaness, Alan (1911–
 *Farewell to the Mountains*. Piano.
Prokofiev, Sergei (1891–1953)
 "The Parting of Romeo and Juliet" from *Romeo and Juliet*. Opus
 64–ter. Orchestral work.
Schumann, Robert (1810–1856)
 "Abschied" (Departure) from *Waldscenen* (Forest scenes). Opus 82.
 Piano.
Wagner, Richard (1813–1883)
 "Wotan's Farewell" from *Die Walküre*. Orchestral work.

## GREECE — see also Greek Myths

Debussy, Claude (1862–1918)
 "Danseuses de Delphes" (Dancing women of Delphi) from *Préludes I*.
 Piano.
 *Prélude à l' après–midi d' un faune* (Prelude to the afternoon of a
 faun). Orchestral work.
Glazunov, Alexander (1865–1936)
 *Overture on Greek Themes*. No. 1. Opus 3. Orchestral work.
 *Overture on Greek Themes*. No. 2. Opus 6. Orchestral work.
Medtner, Nikolai (1880–1951)
 *Dithyrambs*. Opus 10. Piano.
Satie, Erik (1866–1925)
 *Trois Gnossiennes*. Piano.
 *Trois Gymnopédies*. Piano.

# GREEK MYTHS — see also Literature (Aeschylus, Euripides, Sophocles), Muses, Sirens

## ADONIS

Chadwick, George (1854–1931)
*Adonais.* Orchestral work.
Hovhaness, Alan (1911–
*The Garden of Adonis.* Opus 245. Flute and harp.

## HERCULES

Gottschalk, Louis Moreau (1829–1869)
*Hercule.* Opus 88. Piano.
Saint–Saëns, Camille (1835–1921)
*Le Jeunesse d'Hercule* (The youth of Hercules). Opus 50.
Orchestral work.

## JUPITER

Holst, Gustav (1874–1934)
"Jupiter, the Bringer of Jollity" from *The Planets.* Opus 32.
Orchestral work.
Mozart, Wolfgang Amadeus (1756–1791)
Symphony No. 40 in C major *Jupiter.* K. 551.

## MERCURY

Haydn, Franz Joseph (1732–1809)
Symphony No. 43 in E–flat major *Mercury.*
Holst, Gustav (1874–1934)
"Mercury, the Winged Messenger" from *The Planets.* Opus 32.
Orchestral work.

## ORPHEUS

Caccini, Giulio (1545–1618)
*Euridice.* Opera.
Gluck, Christoph Willibald (1714–1787)
*Orfeo ed Euridice.* Opera.
Hovhaness, Alan (1911–
*Meditation on Orpheus.* Orchestral work.
Liszt, Franz (1811–1886)
*Orpheus.* Orchestral work.
Monteverdi, Claudio (1567–1643)
*L'Orfeo.* Opera.

Offenbach, Jacques (1819–1880)
*Orphée aux enfers* (Orpheus in the underworld). Opera.
Schuman, William (1910–
*A Song of Orpheus.* Cello and orchestra.
Stravinsky, Igor (1882–1971)
*Orpheus.* Ballet.

## PAN

Debussy, Claude (1862–1918)
"Pour invoquer Pan, Dieu du vent d'été" (To invoke Pan: God of
the summer wind) from *Six Epigraphes antiques* (Six ancient
inscriptions). Piano duet.
Hanson, Howard (1896–1981)
*Pan and the Priest.* Orchestral work.
Nielsen, Carl (1865–1931)
*Pan and Syrinx.* Opus 49. Orchestral work.

## PENTHESILEA

Goldmark, Carl (1830–1915)
*Penthesilea.* Opus 31. Orchestral work.
Wolf, Hugo (1860–1903)
*Penthesilea.* Orchestral work. Three movements:
(1) "The Departure of Amazons for Troy" (2) "Penthesilea's
Dream of the Feast of the Roses" (3) "Combats, Passions,
Frenzy, Annihilation."

## PROMETHEUS

Beethoven, Ludwig van (1770–1827)
*Die Geschöpfe des Prometheus* (Creatures of Prometheus). Opus
43. Ballet.
Goldmark, Carl (1830–1915)
Overture *Der Gefesselte Prometheus* (Prometheus bound). Opus
38. Orchestral work.
Honegger, Arthur (1892–1955)
*Prométhée.* Incidental music.
Liszt, Franz (1811–1886)
Overture to *Prometheus.* Orchestral work.
Scriabin, Alexander (1872–1915)
*Prometheus: Poem of Fire.* Opus 60. Orchestral work.

## PYGMALION

Rameau, Jean–Philippe (1683–1764)
*Pygmalion.* Opera; ballet.

Suppé, Franz von (1819–1895)
*Die Schöne Galatea* (The beautiful Galatea). Orchestral work.

## VENUS

Chadwick, George (1854–1931)
Overture *Aphrodite*. Orchestral work.
Holst, Gustav (1874–1934)
"Venus, the Bringer of Peace" from *The Planets*. Opus 32.
Orchestral work.
Respighi, Ottorino (1879–1936)
"La Nascita di Venere" (The birth of Venus) from *Trittico
botticelliano* (Botticellian triptych). Orchestral work.
Wagner, Richard (1813–1883)
"Venusberg Music" from *Tannhäuser*. Orchestral work.

## OTHERS

Bliss, Arthur (1891–1975)
*The Olympians*. Opera.
Franck, César (1822–1890)
*Psyché*. Orchestral work. Four movements: (1) "Psyche's Sleep"
(2) "Psyche Borne Away by the Zephyrs" (3) "The Garden of
Eros" (4) "Psyche and Eros."
Holst, Gustav (1874–1934)
*The Planets*. Opus 32. Orchestral work. Seven movements:
(1) "Mars, the Bringer of War" (2) "Venus, the Bringer of
Peace" (3) "Mercury, the Winged Messenger" (4) "Jupiter, the
Bringer of Jollity" (5) "Saturn, the Bringer of Old Age"
(6) "Uranus, the Magician" (7) "Neptune, the Mystic."
Pierné, Gabriel (1863–1937)
*Cydalise et le chèvre–pied* (Cydalise and the satyr). Ballet.
Rameau, Jean–Philippe (1683–1764)
*Castor et Pollux*. Opera.
*Hippolyte et Aricie*. Orchestral work.
Ravel, Maurice (1875–1937)
*Daphnis et Chloé*. Ballet.
Roussel, Albert (1869–1937)
*Bacchus et Ariane*. Opus 43. Ballet.
Strauss, Richard (1864–1949)
*Ariadne auf Naxos* (Ariadne at Naxos). Opera.
Szymanowski, Karol (1882–1937)
*Métopes*. Opus 29. Piano. Three movements: (1) "The Island of
Sirens" (2) "Calypso" (3) "Nausicaa."

## GYPSY

Albéniz, Isaac (1860–1909)
"El Albaicín" from *Iberia,* Book III. Piano.
"Triana" from *Iberia,* Book II. Piano.
Bizet, Georges (1838–1875)
*Carmen.* Opera.
Brahms, Johannes (1833–1897)
*Hungarian Dances* (21). Piano duet; orchestral work.
Falla, Manuel de (1876–1946)
"The Gypsies – Evening" from *El Amor brujo* (Love, the magician).
Ballet.
Ketelbey, Albert (1875–1959)
*Gypsy Lad.* Orchestral work.
Liszt, Franz (1811–1886)
*Hungarian Rhapsodies* (16). Piano.
Ravel, Maurice (1875–1937)
*Tzigane* (Gypsy). Violin and orchestra.
Sarasate, Pablo de (1844–1908)
*Zigeunerweisen* (Gypsy airs). Opus 20, No. 1. Violin and piano.
Strauss, Johann Jr. (1825–1899)
*Der Zigeunerbaron* (The gypsy baron). Opera.
Turina, Joaquín (1882–1949)
*Danzas gitanas* (Gypsy dances). Opus 55. Piano.

# H

HEAVEN — see also Angels

Messiaen, Olivier (1908–
*L'Ascension* (The ascension). Orchestral work. Four movements:
(1) "Majesty of Christ Beseeching His Glory of His Father"
(2) "Serene Hallelujahs of a Soul that Longs for Heaven"
(3) "Hallelujah on the Trumpet, Hallelujah on the Cymbal"
(4) "Prayer of Christ Ascending to His Father."
Wagner, Richard (1813–1883)
"Entrance of the Gods into Valhalla" from *Das Rheingold.*
Orchestral work.

## HELL — see also Devil

Offenbach, Jacques (1819–1880)
*Orphée aux enfers* (Orpheus in the underworld). Opera.
Tchaikovsky, Peter Ilyich (1840–1893)
"Gateway to the Inferno" and "The Turmoil of Hades" from *Francesca da Rimini.* Opus 32. Orchestral work.

## HERO — see also Heroic

Dvorák, Antonín (1841–1904)
*Hero's Song.* Opus 111. Orchestral work.
Strauss, Richard (1864–1949)
*Ein Heldenleben* (A hero's life). Opus 40. Orchestral work.
Six movements: (1) "The Hero" (2) "The Hero's Antagonists"
(3) "The Hero's Helpmate" (4) "The Hero's Battlefield"
(5) "The Hero's Mission of Peace" (6) "The Hero's Escape from the World."

## HEROIC — see also Hero

Beethoven, Ludwig van (1770–1827)
Quartet in C major *Heroic.* Opus 59, No. 3. String quartet.
Symphony No. 3 in E–flat major *Eroica.* Opus 55.
Chopin, Frederic (1810–1849)
Polonaise in A–flat major *Heroic.* Opus 53. Piano.
Glière, Reinhold (1875–1956)
*Heroic March for the Buyiat–Mongolian A.S.S.R.* Opus 71.
Military band.
Liszt, Franz (1811–1886)
"Eroica" from *Etudes d'exécution transcendante* (Transcendental Etudes). Piano.
Schubert, Franz (1797–1828)
*Marches héroïques.* Opus 27. Piano duet.

## HILLS — see also Mountains

Debussy, Claude (1862–1918)
"Les Collines d'Anacapri" (The hills of Anacapri) from *Préludes I.*
Piano.

Delius, Frederick (1862–1934)
  *Over the Hills and Far Away*. Orchestral work.
Harty, Herbert Hamilton (1879–1941)
  "In the Antrim Hills" from *Irish Symphony*.
Siegmeister, Elie (1909–
  "Morning in the Hills" from *Ozark Set*. Orchestral work.


HISTORICAL FIGURES — see also Joan of Arc, Abraham Lincoln, Royalty, Shakespeare

Beethoven, Ludwig van (1770–1827)
  *Coriolan*. Opus 62. Orchestral work.
  *Egmont*. Opus 84. Orchestral work.
Cherubini, Luigi (1760–1842)
  *Epicure* (Epicurus). Opera.
Elgar, Edward (1857–1934)
  *Enigma Variations*. Opus 36. Orchestral work.
Glazunov, Alexander (1865–1936)
  *Stenka Razin*. Opus 13. Orchestral work.
Goldmark, Carl (1830–1915)
  *Sappho*. Opus 44. Orchestral work.
Handel, George Frideric (1685–1759)
  *Giulio Cesare* (Julius Caesar). Opera.
Hanson, Howard (1896–1981)
  *Epilogue to Profiles in Courage: JFK*. Orchestral work.
Hindemith, Paul (1895–1963)
  *Die Harmonie der Welt* (The harmony of the world). Orchestral work.
    Three movements: (1) "Musica Instrumentalis" (2) "Musica
    Humana" (3) "Musica Mundana." (Inspired by Johannes Kepler.)
Meyerbeer, Giacomo (1791–1864)
  *L'Africaine* (The African woman). Opera. (Subtitled "Vasco de
    Gama.")
Milhaud, Darius (1892–1974)
  *Christophe Columb*. Opera.
Moore, Douglas (1893–1969)
  *The Pageant of P.T. Barnum*. Orchestral work. Five movements:
    (1) "Boyhood at Bethal" (2) "Joice Heth" (3) "General & Mrs.
    Tom Thumb" (4) "Jenny Lind" (5) "Circus Parade."
Mussorgsky, Modest (1839–1881)
  *Boris Godunov*. Opera.
  *Ivan the Terrible*. Opus 79. Orchestral work.
Prokofiev, Sergei (1891–1953)
  *Alexander Nevsky*. Opus 78. Orchestral work.
Schönberg, Arnold (1874–1951)
  *Ode to Napoleon*. Opus 41b. Narrator with orchestra.
Shostakovich, Dmitri (1906–1975)
  Symphony No. 12 *Lenin*. Opus 112.

# HOLIDAYS — see also Christmas, Easter

Britten, Benjamin (1913–1976)
*Holiday Dairy.* Opus 5. Four movements: (1) "Early Morning Bathe"
(2) "Sailing" (3) "Fun–Fair" (4) "Night."
Carter, Elliott (1908–
*Holiday Overture.* Orchestral work.
Copland, Aaron (1900–
"Buckaroo Holiday" from *Rodeo.* Ballet; orchestral suite.
Ives, Charles (1874–1954)
*Halloween.* Chamber music.
*Holidays Symphony.* Four movements: (1) "Washington's
Birthday" (2) "Decoration Day" (3) "Fourth of July"
(4) "Thanksgiving or Forefathers' Day."
Turina, Joaquín (1882–1949)
"La Feria" (Holiday) from *Sevilla.* Piano.


# HORSES — see also Animals

Bizet, Georges (1838–1875)
"Les Chevaux de bois" (The merry–go–round) from *Jeux d'enfants*
(Children's games). Piano.
Copland, Aaron (1900–
*The Red Pony.* Orchestral work. Six movements: (1) "Morning on
the Ranch" (2) "The Gift" (3) "Dream March and Circus Music"
(4) "Walk to the Bunkhouse" (5) "Grandfather's Story"
(6) "Happy Ending."
Schumann, Robert (1810–1856)
"Ritter vom Steckenpferd" (Rocking–horse knight) from *Kinderscenen*
(Scenes from childhood). Opus 15. Piano.
"Wilder Reiter" (Wild horseman) from *Album für die Jugend* (Album
for the young). Opus 68. Piano.
Shchedrin, Rodion (1932–
*The Humpbacked Horse.* Ballet.
Villa–Lobos, Heitor (1887–1959)
"Wooden Horse" from *Os animalinhos* (Little toy animals) from *Prole
do bêbê* (Baby's playthings) No. 2. Piano.


# HUMOR — see Clowns, Comedy, Jokes

## HUNGARY

Bartók, Béla (1881–1945)
*Fifteen Hungarian Peasant Songs.* Piano; orchestral work.
"Hungarian Song" from *Mikrokosmos.* Book 3. Piano.
*Improvisations on Hungarian Folk Songs.* Opus 20. Piano.
"In Hungarian Style" from *Mikrokosmos.* Book 2. Piano.
*Mikrokosmos.* Books 1–6. Piano.
*Three Hungarian Folk Songs.* Piano.
Beethoven, Ludwig van (1770–1827)
*König Stephan* (King Stephen). Opus 117. Incidental music.
Brahms, Johannes (1833–1897)
*Hungarian Dances.* Piano duet; orchestral work.
Dohnányi, Ernst (1877–1960)
*Ruralia hungarica.* Opus 33b. Piano; orchestral work.
*Variations on a Hungarian Theme.* Opus 29. Piano.
Kodály, Zoltán (1882–1967)
*Dances of Galánta.* Orchestral work.
*Dances of Marosszék.* Orchestral work.
*Háry János.* Orchestral work. Six movements: (1) "Prelude: The
Fairy Story Begins" (2) "The Viennese Musical Clock" (3) "Song"
(4) "The Battle and Defeat of Napoleon" (5) "Intermezzo"
(6) "Entrance of the Emperor and his Court."
*Variations on a Hungarian Folksong* (Peacock Variations). Orchestral
work.
Liszt, Franz (1811–1886)
*Hungarian Rhapsodies* (16). Piano.

## HUNT

Berlioz, Hector (1803–1869)
"Royal Hunt and Storm" from *Les Troyens* (The Trojans). Orchestral
work.
Byrd, William (1543–1623)
"The Hunt's Up" from *My Ladye Nevells Booke.* Harpsichord.
Clementi, Muzio (1752–1832)
Sonata in D major *La Chasse* (The hunt). Opus 17. Piano.
Franck, César (1822–1890)
*Le Chasseur maudit* (The accursed huntsman). Orchestral work.
Haydn, Franz Joseph (1732–1809)
Quartet No. 1 in B–flat major *La Chasse* (The hunt). Opus 1, No. 1.
Symphony No. 73 in D major *La Chasse* (The hunt).
Liszt, Franz (1811–1886)
"Wilde Jagd" (Wild hunt) from *Etudes d' exécution transcendante*
(Transcendental Etudes). Piano.

Mendelssohn, Felix (1809–1847)
"Jägerlied" (Hunting song) from *Lieder ohne Worte*
(Songs without words). Opus 19. Piano.
Mozart, Wolfgang Amadeus (1756–1791)
Quartet in B–flat major *The Hunt*. K. 458. String quartet.
Prokofiev, Sergei (1891–1953)
Hunter's motif from *Peter and the Wolf*. Narrator and orchestra.
Satie, Erik (1866–1925)
"La Chasse" (The hunt) from *Sports et divertissements* (Sports and
entertainments). Piano.
Schumann, Robert (1810–1856)
"Jäger auf der Lauer" (Hunter in wait) and "Jägdlied" (Hunting song)
from *Waldscenen* (Forest scenes). Opus 82. Piano.
"Jägerliedchen" (Little hunting song) from *Album für die Jugend*
(Album for the young). Opus 68. Piano.
Tchaikovsky, Peter Ilyich (1840–1893)
"September: The Hunt" from *The Seasons*. Opus 37a. Piano.

# I

# INDIA

Delibes, Léo (1836–1891)
*Lakmé*. Opera.
Goldmark, Carl (1830–1915)
*Sakuntala*. Opus 13. Orchestral work.
Holst, Gustav (1874–1934)
*Savitri*. Opus 25. Opera.
MacDowell, Edward (1860–1908)
"The Hindoo Maiden" from *Moon Pictures*. Opus 21. Piano duet.
Rubinstein, Anton (1829–1894)
*Feramors*. Opera.

# INDIANS (American)

Bloch, Ernest (1880–1959)
"1620. The Soil – the Indians – the Mayflower – the Landing
Pilgrims" from *America: An Epic Rhapsody*. Orchestral work.
Busoni, Ferruccio (1866–1924)
*Indianische Fantasie*. Opus 44. Piano and orchestra.
*Indianisches Tagebuch* (Indian diary). Piano.

Castelnuovo–Tedesco, Mario (1895–1968)
*Indian Songs and Dances.* Orchestral work.
Chávez, Carlos (1899–1978)
*Sinfonía India.* Orchestral work.
Coleridge–Taylor, Samuel (1875–1912)
*Hiawatha's Wedding Feast.* Opus 30, No. 1. Orchestral work.
Delius, Frederick (1862–1934)
*Hiawatha.* Orchestral work.
Dvořák, Antonín (1841–1904)
Quartet in F major *American.* Opus 96. String quartet.
Quintet in E–flat major. Opus 97. String quintet.
Symphony No. 9 in E minor *From The New World.* Opus 95.
Goldmark, Rubin (1872–1936)
*Hiawatha.* Orchestral work.
Griffes, Charles Tomlinson (1884–1920)
*Two Sketches on Indian Themes.* String quartet.
Jacobi, Frederick (1891–1952)
*Indian Dances.* Orchestral work.
Quartet No. 1 *American Indian Themes.* String quartet.
MacDowell, Edward (1860–1908)
"From an Indian Lodge" from *Woodland Sketches.* Opus 51. Piano.
"Indian Idyl" from *New England Idyls.* Opus 62. Piano.
Suite No. 2 *Indian.* Opus 48. Orchestral work. Five movements:
(1) "Legend" (2) "Love Song" (3) "In War–time" (4) "Dirge"
(5) "Village Festival."
Skilton, Charles Sanford (1868–1941)
*Two Indian Dances.* String quartet.


INSECTS — see also Butterfly

Bartók, Béla (1881–1945)
"From the Diary of a Fly" from *Mikrokosmos.* Book 6. Piano.
Couperin, François (1631–1701)
*Les Abeilles* (Bees). Ordre 1, No. 8. Harpsichord.
*Les Moucherons* (Flies). Ordre 6, No. 8. Harpsichord.
Elgar, Edward (1857–1934)
"Moths and Butterflies" from *Wand of Youth Suite* No. 2. Opus
1b. Orchestral work.
Liadov, Anatol (1855–1914)
"I Danced With a Mosquito" from *Eight Russian Folksongs.* Opus 58.
Orchestral work.
Rimsky–Korsakov, Nikolai (1844–1908)
"Flight of the Bumblebee" from *The Tale of Tsar Saltan.* Orchestral
work.
Rorem, Ned (1923–
*Spiders.* Harpsichord.

Roussel, Albert (1869–1937)
*Le Festin de l'araignée* (The spider's feast). Opus 17. Ballet.
Five movements: (1) "Prelude" (2) "Entrance of the Ants"
(3) "Dance of the Butterfly" (4) "Hatching and Dance of the
Ephemera" (5) "Funeral March of the Ephemera."
Taylor, Deems (1885–1966)
"Looking Glass Insects" from *Through the Looking Glass.* Orchestral
work.
Villa–Lobos, Heitor (1887–1959)
*Dansa dos mosquitos* (Dance of the Mosquitoes). Orchestral work.


# IRELAND

Bridge, Frank (1879–1941)
*An Irish Melody.* String quartet.
Harty, Herbert Hamilton (1879–1941)
*Irish Symphony.* Four movements: (1) "On the Shores of Lough
Neagh" (2) "The Fair Day" (3) "In the Antrim Hills"
(4) "The Twelfth of July."
Herbert, Victor (1859–1924)
*Irish Rhapsody.* Orchestral work.
Stanford, Charles Villiers (1852–1924)
*Irish Rhapsodies.* Opuses 78, 84, 141, 147. Orchestral work.
Symphony No. 3 in F minor *Irish.* Opus 28.
Sullivan, Arthur (1842–1900)
Symphony in E major *Irish.*


# ISLAND

Bartók, Béla (1881–1945)
"From the Island of Bali" from *Mikrokosmos.* Book 4. Piano.
Bax, Arnold (1883–1953)
*The Garden of Fand.* Orchestral work.
Debussy, Claude (1862–1918)
*L'Isle joyeuse* (The island of joy). Piano.
Gruenberg, Louis (1884–1964)
*The Enchanted Isle.* Orchestral work.
Nielsen, Carl (1865–1931)
*Journey to the Faroe Islands.* Orchestral work.
Rachmaninoff, Sergei (1873–1943)
*Toteninsel* (The isle of the dead). Opus 29. Orchestral work.

Reger, Max (1873–1916)
"Die Toteninsel" (Isle of the dead) from *Vier Tondichtungen nach Arnold Böcklin* (Four tone poems after Arnold Böcklin). Opus 128. Orchestral work.
Revueltas, Silvestre (1899–1940)
*Janitzio.* Orchestral work.
Salzedo, Carlos (1885–1961)
*The Enchanted Isle.* Orchestral work.
Szymanowski, Karol (1882–1937)
"L'Ile des sirènes" (The island of sirens) from *Metopes.* Opus 29. Piano.


ISRAEL — see also Jewish

Bloch, Ernest (1880–1959)
*Israel Symphony.*
Kuhnau, Johann (1660–1722)
"Gideon, Savior of Israel" from *Biblical Sonatas.* Harpsichord.


ITALY — see also Cities (Rome, Venice)

Bach, Johann Sebastian (1685–1750)
Concerto in F major *Italian.* Harpsichord; piano.
Benjamin, Arthur (1893–1960)
*Overture to an Italian Comedy.* Orchestral work.
Berlioz, Hector (1803–1869)
*Harold en Italie* (Harold in Italy). Opus 16. Viola and orchestra.
Four movements: (1) "In the Mountains" (2) "March and Evening Prayer of the Pilgrims" (3) "Serenade of the Mountaineer" (4) "Orgy of the Brigands."
Castelnuovo–Tedesco, Mario (1895–1968)
*Concerto italiano.* Violin and orchestra.
Charpentier, Gustave (1860–1956)
*Impressions d'Italie.* Orchestral work.
Dello Joio, Norman (1913–
"Little Italy" from *New York Profiles.* Orchestral work.
Goldmark, Carl (1830–1915)
*In Italien.* Opus 49. Orchestral work.

Liszt, Franz (1811–1886)
*Années de pèlerinage: Seconde année: Italie* (Years of pilgrimage: second year: Italy). Piano. Seven movements: (1) "Sposalizio" (Wedding) (2) "Il Pensieroso" (The thoughtful one) (3) "Canzonetta del Salvator Rosa" (Song of Salvator Rosa) (4) "Sonetto 47 del Petrarca" (Petrarch sonnet 47) (5) "Sonetto 104 del Petrarca" (Petrarch sonnet 104) (6) "Sonetto 123 del Petrarca" (Petrarch sonnet 123) (7) "Après une lecture de Dante" (After reading Dante).

Mendelssohn, Felix (1809–1847)
Symphony No. 4 in A major *Italian.* Opus 90.

Rossini, Gioacchino (1792–1868)
*L'Italiana in Algeri* (The Italian girl in Algiers). Opera.

Satie, Erik (1866–1925)
"Comédie italienne" (Italian comedy) from *Sports et divertissements* (Sports and entertainments). Piano.

Strauss, Richard (1864–1949)
*Aus Italien* (From Italy). Opus 16. Orchestral work.

Tchaikovsky, Peter Ilyich (1840–1893)
*Capriccio italien.* Opus 45. Orchestral work.
Sextet *Souvenir de Florence* (Recollection of Florence). Opus 70. String sextet.

Tommasini, Vincenzo (1878–1950)
*Paesaggi toscani* (Tuscan landscapes). Orchestral work.

Wolf, Hugo (1860–1903)
*Italian Serenade.* Small orchestra; string quartet.

# J

# JAPAN

Debussy, Claude (1862–1918)
"Pagodes" (Pagodas) from *Estampes* (Engravings). Piano. (Inspired by Japanese prints.)

Holst, Gustav (1874–1934)
*Japanese Suite.* Opus 33. Orchestral work.

Hovhaness, Alan (1911–
*Floating World — Ukiyo.* Opus 209. Orchestral work.
*Fantasy on Japanese Woodprints.* Opus 211. Xylophone and orchestra.

Puccini, Giacomo (1858–1924)
*Madama Butterfly.* Opera.

JESTERS — see Clowns


JEWISH — see also Bible, Israel

Bernstein, Leonard (1918–
  Symphony *Jeremiah*. Mezzo–soprano and orchestra.
Bloch, Ernest (1880–1959)
  *Abodah: a Yom Kippur Melody*. Violin and piano.
  *A Voice in the Wilderness*. Orchestral work.
  *Baal Shem: Three Pictures of Chassidic Life*. Violin and piano.
    Three movements: (1) "Yidui" (Contrition) (2) "Nigun"
    (Improvisation) (3) "Simchas Torah" (Rejoicing).
  *5 Pièces hébraïques* (Five hebrew pieces). Viola and piano.
  *From Jewish Life*. Cello and piano. Three movements: (1) "Prayer"
    (2) "Supplication" (3) "Jewish Song."
  *Israel Symphony*.
  *Trois poèmes juifs* (Three Jewish poems). Orchestral work.
    Three movements: (1) "Danse" (2) "Rite" (3) "Cortège funèbre"
    (Funeral procession).
Bruch, Max (1838–1920)
  *Kol Nidrei*. Opus 47. Cello and orchestra.
Copland, Aaron (1900–
  *Vitebsk, Study on a Jewish Theme*. Violin and piano.
Creston, Paul (1906–1985)
  *Chant of 1942*. Opus 83. Orchestral work.
Jacobi, Frederick (1891–1952)
  *Two Pieces in Sabbath Mood*. Orchestral work.
Milhaud, Darius (1892–1974)
  *Le Candélabre à sept branches* (The seven–branched candelabrum).
    Piano.
Mussorgsky, Modest (1839–1881)
  "Samuel Goldenberg and Schmuyle" from *Pictures at an Exhibition*.
    Piano; orchestral work.
Prokofiev, Sergei (1891–1953)
  *Overture on Hebrew Themes*. Opus 34. Orchestral work.
Shostakovich, Dmitri (1906–1975)
  Symphony No. 13 *Babi Yar*.


## JOAN of ARC

Dello Joio, Norman (1913–
  *The Triumph of St. Joan Symphony*. Three movements:
    (1) "The Maid" (2) "The Warrior" (3) "The Saint."
Honegger, Arthur (1892–1955)
  *Jeanne d'Arc au bûcher* (Joan of Arc at the Stake). Opera.

Rosenthal, Emmanuel (1904–
  *Jeanne d'Arc.* Orchestral work.
Smit, Leo (1921–
  *Joan of Arc.* Orchestral work.
Tchaikovsky, Peter Ilyich (1840–1893)
  *The Maid of Orleans.* Opera.
Verdi, Giuseppe (1813–1901)
  *Giovanna d'Arco* (Joan of Arc). Opera.


JOKES — see also Clowns, Comedy

Haydn, Franz Joseph (1732–1809)
  Quartet No. 38 in E–flat major *The Joke.* Opus 33, No. 2. String
    quartet.
  Symphony No. 94 in G major *Surprise.*
Mozart, Wolfgang Amadeus (1756–1791)
  *Eine Musikalischer Spass* (A musical joke). K. 522. Orchestral work.
Strauss, Johann Jr. (1825–1899)
  *Perpetuum Mobile, musikalischer Scherz* (Perpetual motion, musical
    joke). Opus 257. Orchestral work.
Strauss, Richard (1864–1949)
  *Till Eulenspiegels lustige Streiche* (Till Eulenspiegel's merry
    pranks). Opus 28. Orchestral work.


JOY — see also Affections

Beethoven, Ludwig van (1770–1827)
  Symphony No. 9 in D minor, Movement 4 "Ode to Joy." Opus 125.
  "The Awakening of Joyful Feelings upon Arrival in the Country" from
    Symphony No. 6 in F major *Pastoral.* Opus 68.
Bloch, Ernest (1880–1959)
  "1861 – 1865. Hours of Joy – Hours of Sorrow" from *America:
    An Epic Rhapsody.* Orchestral work.
Chabrier, Emmanuel (1841–1894)
  *Joyeuse Marche.* Orchestral work.
Chadwick, George (1854–1931)
  "Jubilee" from *Symphonic Sketches.* Orchestral work.
Debussy, Claude (1862–1918)
  *L'Isle joyeuse* (The island of joy). Piano.
Hanson, Howard (1896–1981)
  "Joy" from *Four Poems.* Opus 9. Piano.
Hill, Alfred (1870–1960)
  Symphony No. 4 in C minor *Pursuit of Happiness.*

Holst, Gustav (1874–1934)
    "Jupiter, the Bringer of Jollity" from *The Planets*. Opus 32.
    Orchestral work.
Scriabin, Alexander (1872–1915)
    *Poem of Ecstasy*. Opus 54. Orchestral work.
Weber, Carl Maria von (1786–1826)
    *Jubel–Ouvertüre* (Jubilee overture). Opus 59. Orchestral work.

# K

KING ARTHUR LEGENDS — see also Knights, Royalty

Bax, Arnold (1883–1953)
    *Tintagel*. Orchestral work.
Chausson, Ernest (1855–1899)
    *Viviane*. Opus 5. Orchestral work.
Elgar, Edward (1857–1934)
    *King Arthur Suite*. Orchestral work. Six movements:
        (1) "The King and Sir Bedivere" (2) "Elaine Asleep"
        (3) "The Banqueting Hall at Westminster" (4) "The Queen's Tower
    at Night" (5) "Battle Scene" (6) "Arthur's Passage to Avalon."
Goodenberger, Jennifer (1957–
    *Guinevere*. Flute, violin and piano.
Hill, Edward Burlingame (1872–1960)
    *Lancelot and Genevieve*. Orchestral work.
MacDowell, Edward (1860–1908)
    *Lancelot and Elaine*. Opus 25. Orchestral work.
Marty, Georges (1860–1908)
    *Merlin enchanté*. Orchestral work.
Messiaen, Olivier (1908–
    *La Dame de Shalott*. Piano.
Purcell, Henry (1659–1695)
    *King Arthur, or the British Worthy*. Opera.
Rogowski, Ludomir (1881–1954)
    *A Celtic Legend*. Orchestral work. Three movements:
        (1) "Solemn Entrance of the Knights of the Round Table and the
    Oath of King Arthur" (2) "The Dance of Vivian with the Spirits of
    Earth" (3) "Sea–Crossing of Merlin."
Wagner, Richard (1813–1883)
    *Parsifal*. Opera.

KINGS — see King Arthur Legends, Knights, Royalty, Shakespeare

KNIGHTS — see also Don Quixote, King Arthur Legends, Royalty

Bliss, Arthur (1891–1975)
"Dance of the Four Knights," "The Red Knight" and "Death of the Red Knight" from *Checkmate*. Ballet.
Busoni, Ferruccio (1866–1924)
*Zweite Orchester–Suite Geharnischte Suite* [Second orchestral suite (Armor suite)]. Opus 34a. Orchestral work. Four movements: (1) "Vorspiel" (Prelude) (2) "Kriegstanz" (War dance) (3) "Grabdenkmal" (Tombstone) (4) "Ansturm" (Assault).
MacDowell, Edward (1860–1908)
"A Tale of the Knights" from *Three Poems*. Piano duet.
Medtner, Nikolai (1880–1951)
*Knight Errant*. Opus 58, No. 2. Two pianos.
Rogowski, Ludomir (1881–1954)
"Solemn Entrance of the Knights of the Round Table and the Oath of King Arthur" from *A Celtic Legend*. Orchestral work.
Schumann, Robert (1810–1856)
"Knecht Ruprecht" (Knight Rupert) from *Album für die Jugend* (Album for the young). Opus 68. Piano.
"Ritter vom Steckenpferd" (Rocking horse knight) from *Kinderscenen* (Scenes from childhood). Opus 15. Piano.
Strauss, Richard (1864–1949)
*Der Rosenkavalier* (The knight of the rose). Opus 59. Opera.
Taylor, Deems (1885–1966)
"The White Knight" from *Through the Looking Glass*. Orchestral work.
Wagner, Richard (1813–1883)
*Lohengrin*. Opera.

# L

LAKES — see also Water

Brahms, Johannes (1833–1897)
Sonata in A major *Thun* (Lake). Opus 100. Violin and piano.
Carpenter, John Alden (1876–1951)
"The Lake" from *Adventures in a Perambulator*. Orchestral work.
Dvořák, Antonín (1841–1904)
"On the Dark Lake" from *From The Bohemian Forest*. Opus 68. Piano duet.

Griffes, Charles Tomlinson (1884–1920)
*The Lake at Evening.* Orchestral work.
Liadov, Anatol (1855–1914)
*The Enchanted Lake.* Opus 62. Orchestral work.
Liszt, Franz (1811–1886)
"Au lac de Wallenstadt" (By the lake of Wallenstadt) from *Années de pèlerinage: Première année: Suisse* (Years of pilgrimage: first year: Switzerland). Piano.
Tchaikovsky, Peter Ilyich (1840–1893)
*Lac des cygnes* (Swan Lake). Opus 20. Ballet.

## LATIN AMERICA — see also Brazil, Mexico

Barrios, Augustín (1885–1944)
*Danza paraguaya.* Guitar.
Ginastera, Alberto (1916–1983)
*Danzas argentinas.* Piano.
*Twelve American Preludes.* Piano.
Gottschalk, Louis Moreau (1829–1869)
*Columbia, caprice américain.* Opus 34. Piano.
Gould, Morton (1913–
*Latin American Symphonette.* Orchestral work.

## LEAVES — see also Forest, Trees

Debussy, Claude (1862–1918)
"Cloches à travers les feuilles" (Bells through the leaves) from *Images II.* Piano.
"Feuilles mortes" (Dead leaves) from *Préludes II.* Piano.

## LINCOLN, ABRAHAM

Bennett, Robert Russell (1894–1981)
*A Lincoln Symphony.* Four movements: (1) "His Simplicity" (2) "His Affection and his Faith" (3) "His Humor and his Weakness" (4) "His Greatness and his Sacrifice."
Copland, Aaron (1900–
*A Lincoln Portait.* Narrator and orchestra.
Gould, Morton (1913–
*Lincoln Legend.* Orchestral work.

Harris, Roy (1898–1979)
  Symphony No. 6 *Gettysburg Address*. Four movements:
    (1) "Awakening" (2) "Conflict" (3) "Dedication"
    (4) "Admiration."
  Symphony No. 10 *Abraham Lincoln*. Five movements:
    (1) "Lonesome Boy in the Wilderness" (2) "The Young Wrestler"
    (3) "Abraham Lincoln's Conviction" (4) "Civil War, Brother
    against Brother" (5) "Praise and Thanksgiving for Peace."
Mason, Daniel Gregory (1873–1953)
  Symphony No. 3 *Lincoln*. Opus 35. Four movements:
    (1) "The Candidate from Springfield" (2) "Massa Linkum"
    (3) "Old Abe's Yans" (4) "1865."
Weinberger, Jaromir (1896–1967)
  *Abraham Lincoln Symphony*.


LITERATURE — see also Don Quixote, Faust, Greek Myths,
              Shakespeare

  (Composers listed alphabetically after author)

AESCHYLUS

Goldmark, Carl (1830–1915)
  *Der gefesselte Prometheus* (Prometheus bound). Opus 38.
    Orchestral work.
Honegger, Arthur (1892–1955)
  *Prométhée*. Incidental music.
Milhaud, Darius (1892–1974)
  *L'Orestie*. Opus 24. Opera trilogy. (1) "Agamemnon"
    (2) "Les Choëphores" (The libation bearers)
    (3) "Les Euménides."
Stanford, Charles Villiers (1852–1924)
  *The Eumenides*. Opus 23. Incidental music.

ALCOTTS

Ives, Charles (1874–1954)
  "The Alcotts" from Sonata No. 2 *Concord*. Piano.

ANDERSEN, HANS CHRISTIAN

MacDowell, Edward (1860–1908)
  *Moon Pictures*. Opus 21. Piano duet. Five movements:
    (1) "The Hindoo Maiden" (2) "Stork's Story" (3) "In Tyrol"
    (4) "The Swan" (5) "Visit of the Bear." (Inspired by Hans
    Christian Andersen.)

Stravinsky, Igor (1882–1971)
*Le Baiser de la fée* (The fairy's kiss). Ballet.
*Le Chant du rossignol* (The song of the nightingale). Ballet;
orchestral work. Three movements: (1) "The Palace of the
Chinese Emperor" (2) "The Two Nightingales" (3) "Illness
and Recovery of the Chinese Emperor."
*Le Rossignol* (The nightingale). Opera.

## ARABIAN NIGHTS

Rabaud, Henri (1873–1949)
*Mârouf.* Opera.
Rimsky–Korsakov, Nikolai (1844–1908)
*Scheherazade.* Opus 35. Orchestral work. Four movements:
(1) "The Sea and Sinbad's Ship" (2) "The Kalendar Prince"
(3) "The Young Prince" (4) "Festival at Baghdad – The Sea –
The Ship Founders on the Rock."
Strauss, Johann Jr. (1825–1899)
*Tausend und eine Nacht* (A thousand and one nights). Opus 346.
Waltz.
Weber, Carl Maria von (1786–1826)
*Abu Hassan.* Opera.

## ARISTOPHANES

Auric, Georges (1899–1983)
*The Birds.* Incidental music.
Bernstein, Leonard (1918–
"Aristophanes" from *Serenade for Violin, Strings and Percussion.*
Ornstein, Leo (1892–
*Lysistrata.* Orchestral work.
Vaughan Williams, Ralph (1872–1958)
*The Wasps.* Orchestral work.

## AUDEN, WYSTAN HUGH

Bernstein, Leonard (1918–
Symphony *The Age of Anxiety.* Piano and orchestra.

## BARRIE, JAMES

Davies, Henry Walford (1869–1941)
*Peter Pan.* Opus 30. String quartet.

## BRONTE, EMILY

Floyd, Carlisle (1926–
*Wuthering Heights.* Opera.

## BROWNING, ROBERT

Ives, Charles (1874–1954)
*Robert Browning Overture.* Orchestral work.

## BURNS, ROBERT

Chadwick, George (1854–1931)
*Tam O'Shanter.* Orchestral work.
Mackenzie, Alexander (1847–1935)
Scottish Rhapsody No. 2 *Burns.* Opus 24. Orchestral work.
Scottish Rhapsody No. 3 *Tam O'Shanter.* Opus 74. Orchestral work.

## BYRON,GEORGE GORDON, LORD

Berlioz, Hector (1803–1869)
*Harold en Italie* (Harold in Italy). Opus 16. Viola and orchestra. Four movements: (1) "In the Mountains" (2) "March and Evening Prayer of the Pilgrims" (3) "Serenade of the Mountaineer" (4) "Orgy of the Brigands."
*Le Corsaire.* Opus 21. Orchestral work.
Liszt, Franz (1811–1886)
*Tasso.* Orchestral work.
Schönberg, Arnold (1874–1951)
*Ode to Napoleon.* Opus 41b. Narrator and orchestra.
Schumann, Robert (1810–1856)
*Manfred.* Opus 115. Orchestral work.
Tchaikovsky, Peter Ilyich (1840–1893)
Symphony *Manfred.* Opus 58.

## CARROLL, LEWIS

Kelley, Edgar Stillman (1857–1944)
*Alice in Wonderland.* Orchestral work.
Taylor, Deems (1885–1966)
*Through the Looking Glass.* Orchestral work. Four movements: (1) "Dedication: The Garden of Live Flowers" (2) "Jabberwocky" (3) "Looking Glass Insects" (4) "The White Knight."

## CERVANTES — see Don Quixote

## CLAUDEL, PAUL

Milhaud, Darius (1892–1974)
*Symphony Suite No. 2 Protée.* Opus 57. Orchestral work.

## COLERIDGE, SAMUEL TAYLOR

Griffes, Charles Tomlinson (1884–1920)
*The Pleasure Dome of Kubla Khan.* Orchestral work.

## DANTE ALIGHIERI

Foote, Arthur (1853–1937)
*Francesca da Rimini.* Opus 24. Orchestral work.
Granados, Enrique (1867–1916)
*La Divina commedia.* Orchestral work.
Liszt, Franz (1811–1886)
"Après une lecture du Dante" (After reading Dante) from *Années de pèlerinage: Seconde année: Italie* (Years of pilgrimage: second year: Italy). Piano.
*Dante Symphony.*
Tchaikovsky, Peter Ilyich (1840–1893)
*Francesca da Rimini.* Opus 32. Orchestral work.
Three movements: (1) "Introduction: The Gateway to the Inferno, Tortures of the Condemned" (2) "Francesca Tells the Story of her Tragic Love for Paolo" (3) "The Turmoil of Hades, Conclusion."

## DICKENS, CHARLES

Debussy, Claude (1862–1918)
"Hommage à S. Pickwick, Esq." from *Préludes II.* Piano.

## ELIOT, T.S.

Milhaud, Darius (1892–1974)
*Murder in the Cathedral.* Incidental music.
Pizzetti, Ildebrando (1880–1968)
*Assassinio nella catedrale* (Murder in the cathedral). Opera.

## EURIPIDES — see also Greek Myths

Barber, Samuel (1910–1981)
*Medea (The Cave of the Heart).* Opus 23. Ballet.
Cherubini, Luigi (1760–1842)
*Iphigenia in Aulis.* Opera.
*Médée.* Opera.

Gluck, Christoph Willibald (1714–1787)
*Iphigenia en Aulide.* Opera.
*Iphigenia en Tauride.* Opera.
Indy, Vincent d' (1851–1931)
*Médée.* Opus 47. Incidental music.
Milhaud, Darius (1892–1974)
*Hécuba.* Incidental music.
Mitropoulos, Dimitros (1896–1960)
*Electra.* Incidental music.
*Hippolytus.* Incidental music.
Piccinni, Niccolò (1728–1800)
*Iphigénia en Tauride.* Opera.
Thomson, Virgil (1896–
*The Trojan Women.* Incidental music.

FITZGERALD, EDWARD

Foote, Arthur (1853–1937)
*Four Character Pieces after Omar Khayyám.* Opus 48. Orchestral
work.
Hovhaness, Alan (1911–
*Rubáiyát of Omar Khayyám.* Orchestral work.

GOETHE, JOHANN WOLFGANG VON — see also Faust

Beethoven, Ludwig van (1770–1827)
*Egmont.* Opus 84. Orchestral work.
Dukas, Paul (1865–1935)
*L'Apprenti sorcier* (The sorcerer's apprentice). Orchestral work.
MacDowell, Edward (1860–1908)
*Six Idyls after Goethe.* Opus 28. Piano. Six movements:
(1) "In the Woods" (2) "Siesta" (3) "To the Moonlight"
(4) "Silver Clouds" (5) "Flute Idyl" (6) "The Bluebell."
Massenet, Jules (1842–1912)
*Werther.* Opera. [Inspired by *Die Leiden des Jungen Werthers*
(The sorrows of young Werther)].
Mendelssohn, Felix (1809–1847)
*Meeresstille und glückliche Fahrt* (Calm sea and prosperous
voyage). Opus 27. Orchestral work.
Schumann, Robert (1810–1856)
*Hermann und Dorothea.* Opus 136. Orchestral work.

GRAHAME, KENNETH

Thompson, Randall (1899–1984)
*The Wind in the Willows.* String quartet.

## HARDY, THOMAS

Holst, Gustav (1874–1934)
*Egdon Heath.* Orchestral work. (Inspired by *Return of the Native.*)

## HAWTHORNE, NATHANIEL

Hanson, Howard (1896–1981)
*Merry Mount.* Opus 31. Opera; orchestral work.
Ives, Charles (1874–1954)
"Hawthorne" from Sonata No. 2 *Concord.* Piano.

## HEINE, HEINRICH

MacDowell, Edward (1860–1908)
*Six Poems after Heine.* Opus 31. Piano. Six movements:
(1) "From a Fisherman's Hut" (2) "Scotch Poem" (3) "From Long Ago" (4) "The Post Wagon" (5) "The Shepherd Boy" (6) "Monologue."

## HOLBERG, LUDVIG

Grieg, Edvard (1843–1907)
*Holberg Suite.* Opus 40. String orchestra.

HOMER — see also Greek Myths

Fauré, Gabriel (1845–1924)
*Pénélope.* Orchestral work.
Hadley, Henry (1871–1937)
*Hector and Andromache.* Orchestral work.
Hovhanness, Alan
Symphony No. 25 *Odysseus.* Opus 275.
Jacobi, Frederick (1891–1952)
Impressions from the *Odyssey.* Violin and piano.
Szymanowski, Karol (1882–1937)
*Metopes.* Opus 29. Piano. Three movements:
(1) "L'Ile des sirènes" (The island of the sirens) (2) "Calypso" (3) "Nausicaa."

## HUGO, VICTOR

Delibes, Léo (1836–1891)
*Ruy Blas.* Orchestral work.

Franck, César (1822–1890)
*Ce qu' on entend sur la montagne* (What one hears on the mountain). Orchestral work.
Liszt, Franz (1811–1886)
*Ce qu' on entend sur la montagne.* Orchestral work.
*Mazeppa.* Orchestral work.
MacDowell, Edward (1860–1908)
*Les Orientales.* Opus 37. Piano. Three movements: (1) "Clair de lune" (Moonlight) (2) "Dans le hamac" (In the hammock) (3) "Danse andalouse" (Andalusian dance).
Massenet, Jules (1842–1912)
*Nôtre–Dame de Paris.* Incidental music.
Mendelssohn, Felix (1809–1847)
*Ruy Blas.* Opus 95. Orchestral work.

IBSEN, HENRIK

Grieg, Edvard (1843–1907)
*Peer Gynt.* Suite No. 1. Opus 46. Orchestral work.
Four movements: (1) "Morning" (2) "Åse's Death" (3) "Anitra's Dance" (4) "In the Hall of the Mountain King."
*Peer Gynt.* Suite No. 2. Opus 55. Orchestral work.
Four movements: (1) "The Abduction and Ingrid's Lament" (2) "Arab Dance" (3) "Peer Gynt's Homecoming" (4) "Solveig's Song."

IRVING, WASHINGTON

Chadwick, George (1854–1931)
*Rip Van Winkle.* Orchestral work.
Weinberger, Jaromir (1896–1967)
*The Legend of Sleepy Hollow.* Orchestral work.
Four movements: (1) "Sleepy Hollow" (2) "Katrina's Waltz" (3) "The Headless Horseman and Ichabod Crane" (4) "Dutch Polka."

JAMES, HENRY

Britten, Benjamin (1913–1976)
*The Turn of the Screw.* Opera.

KEATS, JOHN

MacDowell, Edward (1860–1908)
*Lamia.* Opus 29. Orchestral work.

## LAMARTINE

Liszt, Franz (1811–1886)
*Les Préludes.* Orchestral work.

## LENAU, NIKOLAUS

Liszt, Franz (1811–1886)
*Faust.* Orchestral work.
*Mephisto Waltz.* Orchestral work.

## LONGFELLOW, HENRY WADSWORTH

Coleridge–Taylor, Samuel (1875–1912)
*Hiawatha's Wedding Feast.* Opus 30, No. 1. Orchestral work.
Delius, Frederick (1862–1934)
*Hiawatha.* Orchestral work.
Goldmark, Rubin (1872–1936)
*Hiawatha.* Orchestral work.

## MAETERLINCK, MAURICE

Debussy, Claude (1862–1918)
*Pelléas et Mélisande.* Opera.
Fauré, Gabriel (1845–1924)
*Pelléas et Mélisande.* Opus 80. Orchestral work.
Four movements: (1) "Prelude" (2) "Les Fileuses" (The
spinner) (3) "Siciliana" (4) "The Death of Mélisande."
Honegger, Arthur (1892–1955)
*Aglavaine et Sélysette.* Orchestral work.
Loeffler, Charles Martin (1861–1935)
*La Mort de Tintagiles* (The death of Tintagiles). Orchestral work.
Schönberg, Arnold (1874–1951)
*Pelleas und Melisande.* Opus 5. Orchestral work.
Sibelius, Jean (1865–1957)
*Pelléas et Mélisande.* Opus 46. Orchestral work.
Nine movements: (1) "At the Castle Gate" (2) "Mélisande"
(3) "By the Sea" (4) "A Fountain in the Park" (5) "The Three
Blind Sisters" (6) "Pastorale" (7) "Mélisande at the Spinning
Wheel" (8) "Entr'acte" (9) "Death of Mélisande."

## MALLARME, STEPHANE

Debussy, Claude (1862–1918)
*Prélude à l'après–midi d'un faune* (Prelude to the afternoon of a
faun). Orchestral work.

Hindemith, Paul (1895–1963)
*Hérodiade*. Orchestral work.
Ravel, Maurice (1875–1937)
*Trois poèmes de Stéphane Mallarmé* (Three poems by Stéphane
Mallarmé). Chamber music.

## MANN, THOMAS

Britten, Benjamin (1913–1976)
*Death in Venice*. Opus 88. Opera.

## MELVILLE, HERMAN

Britten, Benjamin (1913–1976)
*Billy Budd*. Opera.

## MILLER, ARTHUR

Ward, Robert (1917–
*The Crucible*. Opera.

## MOLIERE

Auric, Georges (1899–1983)
*Les Fâcheux* (The bore). Incidental music.
Lully, Jean–Baptiste (1632–1687)
*George Dandin*. Incidental music.
*L'Amour médecin* (Love, the physician). Incidental music.
Strauss, Richard (1864–1949)
*Le Bourgeois gentilhomme*. Opus 66. Orchestral work.
Nine movements: (1) "Overture" (2) "Minuet"
(3) "The Fencing Master" (4) "Entrance and Dance of the
Tailors" (5) "The Minuet of Lully" (6) "Courante"
(7) "Entrance of Cleonte" (8) "Intermezzi: Dorante and
Dorimente, Count and Marquise" (9) "The Dinner."

## NIETZSCHE, FRIEDRICH WILHELM

Strauss, Richard (1864–1949)
*Also sprach Zarathustra* (Thus spoke Zarathustra). Opus 30.
Orchestral work.

## OVID

Britten, Benjamin (1913–1976)
*Six Metamorphoses after Ovid*. Opus 49. Oboe.

## PETRARCH (FRANCESCO PETRARCA)

Liszt, Franz (1811–1886)
"Sonettos 47, 104, 123 del Petrarca" (Petrarch sonnets) from *Années de pèlerinage: Seconde année: Italie* (Years of pilgrimage: second year: Italy). Piano.
Schönberg, Arnold (1874–1951)
*Serenade.* 4th Movement. Opus 24. Chamber music.

## PLATO

Bernstein, Leonard (1918–
*Serenade for Violin, Strings and Percussion* (Plato's Symposium). Five movements: (1) "Phaedrus" (2) "Eryximachus" (3) "Aristophanes" (4) "Alcibiades" (5) "Socrates."

## POE, EDGAR ALLAN

Caplet, André (1878–1925)
*Conte fantastique.* Harp and strings.
*Le Masque de la mort rouge* (The Masque of the Red Death). Orchestral work.
Gilbert, Henry F. (1868–1928)
*The Island of the Fay.* Piano.
Holbrooke, Joseph (1878–1958)
*Israfel.* Opus 33. Wind instruments and piano.
*The Masque of the Red Death.* Orchestral work.
*Ulalume.* Orchestral work.
Kelley, Edgar Stillman (1857–1944)
*The Pit and the Pendulum.* Orchestral work.
Miaskovsky, Nikolai (1881–1950)
*Nevermore.* Opus 9. Orchestral work.
Schmitt, Florent (1870–1958)
*Le Palais hanté* (The haunted place). Opus 49. Orchestral work.

## PUSHKIN, ALEXANDER

Liadov, Anatol (1855–1914)
*Polonaise in Memory of Pushkin.* Opus 49. Orchestral work.
Mussorgsky, Modest (1839–1881)
*Boris Godunov.* Opera.
Prokofiev, Sergei (1891–1953)
*Boris Godunov.* Opus 74. Incidental music.
*Eugene Onegin.* Opus 71. Incidental music.
Shebalin, Vissarion (1902–1963)
*Mozart and Salieri.* Incidental music.
Tchaikovsky, Peter Ilyich (1840–1893)
*Eugene Onegin.* Opus 24. Opera.

## RACINE

Mendelssohn, Felix (1809–1847)
"War March of the Priests" from *Athalie*. Opus 74. Orchestral
work.

## SCHILLER, FRIEDRICH VON

Beethoven, Ludwig van (1770–1827)
Symphony No. 9 in D minor, Movement 4 "Ode to Joy." Opus
125.
Indy, Vincent d' (1851–1931)
*Wallenstein*. Opus 12. Three symphonic overtures:
(1) "Le Camp" (2) "Max et Thécla" (3) "La Mort de
Wallenstein" (The death of Wallenstein).
Liszt, Franz (1811–1886)
*Die Ideale*. Orchestral work.
Rheinberger, Joseph (1839–1901)
*Demetrius*. Opus 110. Orchestral work.
*Wallenstein*. Opus 10. Orchestral work.
Rossini, Gioacchino (1792–1868)
*Guillaume Tell* (William Tell). Opera.
Schumann, Robert (1810–1856)
*Die Braut von Messina* (The bride from Messina). Opus 100.
Orchestral work.
Smetana, Bedrich (1824–1884)
*Wallenstein's Camp*. Orchestral work.

## SCOTT, WALTER

Barnett, John Francis (1837–1916)
*The Lay of the Last Minstrel*. Orchestral work.
Berlioz, Hector (1803–1869)
*Rob Roy*. Orchestral work.
*Waverly*. Opus 2. Orchestral work.
Donizetti, Gaetano (1797–1848)
*Lucia di Lammermoor*. Opera. (Inspired by *The Bride of
Lammermoor*.)
Sullivan, Arthur (1842–1900)
*Ivanhoe*. Opera.
*Marmion*. Orchestral work.

## SHELLEY, PERCY BYSSHE

Barber, Samuel (1910–1981)
*Music for a Scene from Shelley*. Opus 7. Orchestral work.
Chadwick, George (1854–1931)
*Adonais*. Orchestral work.

MacDowell, Edward (1860–1908)
"Winter" from *Four Little Poems*. Opus 32. Piano.

## SHERIDAN, RICHARD BRINSLEY

Barber, Samuel (1910–1981)
*The School for Scandal*. Opus 5. Orchestral work.
Kabalevsky, Dmitri (1904–1987)
*The School for Scandal*. Incidental music.

## SOCRATES

Bernstein, Leonard (1918–
"Socrates" from *Serenade for Violin, Strings and Percussion*
(Plato's Symposium).

## SOPHOCLES

Bantock, Granville (1868–1946)
*Oedipus Coloneus–Overture to a Greek Tragedy*. Orchestral work.
Chávez, Carlos (1899–1978)
*Sinfonía de Antígona*. Orchestral work.
Gabrieli, Andrea (1510–1586)
*Oedipus Tyrannus*. Incidental music.
Glière, Reinhold (1875–1956)
*Oedipus Rex*. Incidental music.
Honegger, Arthur (1892–1955)
*Antigone*. Opera.
*Oedipus Rex*. Incidental music.
Mendelssohn, Felix (1809–1847)
*Antigone*. Opus 55. Incidental music.
*Oedipus at Colonus*. Opus 93. Incidental music.
Orff, Carl (1895–1982)
*Antigonae*. Opera.
Paine, John Knowles (1839–1906)
*Oedipus Tyrannus*. Opus 35.
Orchestral work.
Saint–Saëns, Camille (1835–1921)
*Antigone*. Incidental music.
Strauss, Richard (1864–1949)
*Elektra*. Opus 58. Opera.
Stravinsky, Igor (1882–1971)
*Oedipus Rex*. Opera–oratorio.
Thomson, Virgil (1896–
*Oedipus Tyrannus*. Incidental music.

## STEINBECK, JOHN

Copland, Aaron (1900–
*The Red Pony.* Orchestral work. Six movements:
(1) "Morning on the Ranch" (2) "The Gift" (3) "Dream March
and Circus Music" (4) "Walk to the Bunkhouse"
(5) "Grandfather's Story" (6) "Happy Ending."

## TENNYSON, ALFRED, LORD

MacDowell, Edward (1860–1908)
*Lancelot and Elaine.* Opus 25. Orchestral work. (Inspired by
*Idyls of the King.*)
"The Eagle" from *Four Little Poems.* Opus 32. Piano.
Messiaen, Olivier (1908–
*La Dame de Shalott.* Piano.
Stanford, Charles Villiers (1852–1924)
*Becket.* Opus 48. Incidental music.
*Queen Mary.* Opus 6. Incidental music.

## THOREAU, HENRY DAVID

Ives, Charles (1874–1954)
"Thoreau" from Sonata No. 2 *Concord.* Piano.
Mason, Daniel Gregory (1873–1953)
*Chanticleer.* Orchestral work.

## TOLSTOY, LEO

Janácek, Leos (1854–1928)
Quartet No. 1. (Inspired by *The Kreutzer Sonata.*) String quartet.
Prokofiev, Sergei (1891–1953)
*War and Peace.* Opus 91. Opera.
Roussel, Albert (1869–1937)
*Résurrection.* Opus 4. Orchestral work.

## TWAIN, MARK

Grofé, Ferde (1892–1972)
"Huckleberry Finn" from *Mississippi Suite.* Orchestral work.

## VERLAINE, PAUL

Fauré, Gabriel (1845–1924)
*Masques et bergamasques.* Opus 112. Orchestral work.
Loeffler, Charles Martin (1861–1935)
*La Bonne chanson* (The beautiful song). Orchestral work.

## VIRGIL

Loeffler, Charles Martin (1861–1935)
*A Pagan Poem*. Opus 14. Orchestral work.

## VOLTAIRE

Bernstein, Leonard (1918–
*Candide*. Opera.

## WHITMAN, WALT

Carpenter, John Alden (1876–1951)
*Sea Drift*. Orchestral work.
Converse, Frederick (1871–1940)
*The Mystic Trumpeter*. Opus 19. Orchestral work.
Holst, Gustav (1874–1934)
*Walt Whitman*. Opus 7. Orchestral work.

## WILDE, OSCAR

Carpenter, John Alden (1876–1951)
*The Birthday of the Infanta*. Ballet. Three movements:
    (1) "The Guest" (2) "The Infanta" (3) "The Games."
Castelnuovo–Tedesco, Mario (1895–1968)
*The Birthday of the Infanta*. Ballet. Seven movements:
    (1) "Fanfare" (2) "Sarabande of the King of Spain"
    (3) "Pavane of the Infanta" (4) "Ronde of Las Meninas"
    (5) "Minuet of the Rose" (6) "Dance of the Mirror"
    (7) "Epilogue."
Ibert, Jacques (1890–1962)
*Ballade de la geôle de Reading* (The ballad of Reading Gaol).
    Ballet.
Strauss, Richard (1864–1949)
*Salome*. Opus 54. Opera.

## WILDER, THORNTON

Copland, Aaron (1900–
*Our Town*. Orchestral work.

LOVE — see also Don Juan, Lovers, Marriage

Berlioz, Hector (1803–1869)
*Symphonie fantastique* (Fantastic symphony). Opus 14.
Five movements: (1) "Dreams, Passions" (2) "The Ball"
(3) "Scene in the Country" (4) "March to the Gallows"
(5) "Dream of the Witches' Sabbath."
Bernstein, Leonard (1918–
*Serenade for Violin, Strings and Percussion* (Plato's Symposium).
Five movements: (1) "Phaedrus" (2) "Eryximachus"
(3) "Aristophanes" (4) "Alcibiades" (5) "Socrates."
"The Great Lover" from *On the Town.* Orchestral work.
Donizetti, Gaetano (1797–1848)
*L'Elisir d'amore* (The love potion). Opera.
Falla, Manuel de (1876–1946)
*El Amor brujo* (Love, the magician). Ballet. Twelve movements:
(1) "Introduction and Scene" (2) "The Gypsies – Evening"
(3) "Scene of Sorrowing Love" (4) "The Homecomer" (5) "Dance
of Terror" (6) "The Magic Circle" (7) "Ritual Fire Dance"
(8) "Scene" (9) "Song of the Will–o'–the–Wisp"
(10) "Pantomime" (11) "Dance of the Game of Love"
(12) "Morning Chimes."
Granados, Enrique (1867–1916)
"El Amor y la muerte" (Love and death) from *Goyescas.* Piano.
Hanson, Howard (1896–1981)
"Love Duet" from *Merry Mount.* Opus 31. Opera; orchestral work.
Indy, Vincent d' (1851–1931)
"Amour" (Love) from *Poème des montagnes* (Poem of the mountains).
Opus 15. Piano.
Janácek, Leos (1854–1928)
Quartet No. 2 *Intimate Pages.* String quartet.
Liszt, Franz (1811–1886)
*Liebesträume* (Love's dream). Piano.
Lully, Jean–Baptiste (1632–1687)
*L'Amour médecin* (Love, the physician). Incidental music.
Wagner, Richard (1813–1883)
"Vorspiel und Liebestod" (Prelude and love–death) from *Tristan und
Isolde.* Orchestral work.

LOVERS — see also Love, Marriage

Berlioz, Hector (1803–1869)
*Béatrice et Bénédict.* Opera.
*Roméo et Juliette.* Opus 17. Symphonic work with voice.
Debussy, Claude (1862–1918)
*Pelléas et Mélisande.* Opera.

Delius, Frederick (1862–1934)
*A Village Romeo and Juliet.* Opera.
Diamond, David (1915–
*Romeo and Juliet.* Orchestral work. Five movements: (1) "Overture" (2) "Balcony Scene" (3) "Romeo and Friar Laurence" (4) "Juliet and her Nurse" (5) "Death of Romeo and Juliet."
Fauré, Gabriel (1845–1924)
*Pelléas et Mélisande.* Opus 80. Incidental music. Four movements: (1) "Prelude" (2) "The Spinner" (3) "Siciliana" (4) "The Death of Mélisande."
Franck, César (1822–1890)
*Psyché.* Orchestral work. Four movements: (1) "Psyche's Sleep" (2) "Psyche Borne Away by the Zephyrs" (3) "The Garden of Eros" (4) "Psyche and Eros."
Gershwin, George (1898–1937)
*Porgy and Bess.* Opera.
Gluck, Christoph Willibald (1714–1787)
*Orfeo ed Euridice.* Opera.
MacDowell, Edward (1860–1908)
*Lancelot and Elaine.* Opus 25. Orchestral work.
Monteverdi, Claudio (1567–1643)
*L'Incoronazione di Poppea* (The coronation of Poppea). Opera.
Mozart, Wolfgang Amadeus (1756–1791)
*Bastien und Bastienne.* K. 50. Opera.
Prokofiev, Sergei (1891–1953)
*Romeo and Juliet.* Opus 64–bis. Ballet. Seven movements: (1) "Dance of the People" (2) "Scene" (3) "Madrigal" (4) "Minuet" (5) "Masques" (6) "Romeo and Juliet" (7) "The Death of Tybalt."
*Romeo and Juliet.* Opus 64–ter. Ballet. Seven movements: (1) "Montagues and Capulets" (2) "Juliet, the Maiden" (3) "Friar Laurence" (4) "Dance" (5) "The Parting of Romeo and Juliet" (6) "Dance of the West Indian Slave Girls" (7) "Romeo at Juliet's Grave."
*Romeo and Juliet.* Opus 101. Ballet. Six movements: (1) "Romeo at the Fountain" (2) "The Morning Dance" (3) "Juliet" (4) "The Nurse" (5) "Morning Serenade" (6) "Juliet's Death."
Purcell, Henry (1659–1695)
*Dido and Aeneas.* Opera.
Ravel, Maurice (1875–1937)
*Daphnis et Chloé.* Ballet.
Rorem, Ned (1923–
*Romeo and Juliet.* Flute and guitar.
Saint–Saëns, Camille (1835–1921)
*Samson et Dalila.* Opus 47. Opera.
Schönberg, Arnold (1874–1951)
*Pelleas und Melisande.* Opus 5. Orchestral work.
*Verklärte Nacht* (Transfigured night). Opus 4. String sextet; string orchestra.

Sibelius, Jean (1865–1957)
*Pelléas et Mélisande.* Opus 46. Orchestral work. Nine movements:
(1) "At the Castle Gate" (2) "Mélisande" (3) "By the Sea"
(4) "A Fountain in the Park" (5) "The Three Blind Sisters"
(6) "Pastorale" (7) "Mélisande at the Spinning Wheel"
(8) "Entr'acte" (9) "Death of Mélisande."
Strauss, Richard (1864–1949)
"The Hero's Helpmate" from *Ein Heldenleben* (A hero's life).
Opus 40. Orchestral work.
Tchaikovsky, Peter Ilyich (1840–1893)
*Francesca da Rimini.* Opus 32. Orchestral work. Three movements:
(1) "Introduction: The Gateway to the Inferno, Tortures of the
Condemned" (2) "Francesca Tells the Story of her Tragic Love for
Paolo" (3) "The Turmoil of Hades, Conclusion."
*Romeo and Juliet.* Orchestral work.
Tcherepnin, Alexander (1899–1977)
"Chota and Thamar" from *Georgiana.* Opus 92. Piano and strings.
Wagner, Richard (1813–1883)
*Tristan und Isolde.* Opera.
Walton, William (1902–1983)
*Troilus and Cressida.* Opera.


LULLABY — see also Sleep

Grieg, Edvard (1843–1907)
"Cradle Song" from *Lyric Pieces.* Opus 68, No. 5. Piano; orchestral
work.
Khachaturian, Aram (1903–1978)
"Lullaby" from *Gayane.* Suite No. 1. Ballet.
Liadov, Anatol (1855–1914)
"Cradle Song" from *Eight Russian Folksongs.* Opus 58. Orchestral
work.


# M


MACHINES — see also Spinning Wheel

Anderson, Leroy (1908–1975)
*Typewriter.* Orchestral work.
Antheil, George (1900–1959)
*Ballet mécanique.* Ballet.

Couperin, François (1631–1701)
*Les Petits moulins à vent* (The little windmills). Ordre 17, No. 3.
Harpsichord.
Liszt, Franz (1811–1886)
"Chasse–neige" (Snow plough) from *Etudes d'exécution transcendante*
(Transcendental Etudes). Piano.
Menotti, Gian–Carlo (1911–
*The Telephone.* Opera.
Prokofiev, Sergei (1891–1953)
*Le Pas d'acier* (The age of steel). Opus 41a. Ballet. Six movements:
(1) "Train of Men Carrying Bags" (2) "Sailor with Bracelet and
Working Women" (3) "Reconstruction of Scenery"
(4) "The Factory" (5) "The Hammer" (6) "The Final Scene."
Schuller, Gunther (1925–
"The Twittering Machine" from *Seven Studies on Themes of Paul
Klee.* Orchestral work.


## MAGIC and MAGICIANS

Dukas, Paul (1865–1935)
*L'Apprenti sorcier* (The sorcerer's apprentice). Orchestral work.
Falla, Manuel de (1876–1946)
*El Amor brujo* (Love, the magician). Ballet. Twelve movements:
(1) "Introduction and Scene" (2) "The Gypsies – Evening"
(3) "Scene of Sorrowing Love" (4) "The Homecomer"
(5) "Dance of Terror" (6) "The Magic Circle" (7) "Ritual Fire
Dance" (8) "Scene" (9) "Song of the Will–o'–the–Wisp"
(10) "Pantomime" (11) "Dance of the Game of Love"
(12) "Morning Chimes."
Holst, Gustav (1874–1934)
"Uranus, the Magician" from *The Planets.* Opus 32. Orchestral work.
Mozart, Wolfgang Amadeus (1756–1791)
*Die Zauberflöte* (The magic flute). K. 620. Opera.
Ravel, Maurice (1875–1937)
*L'Enfant et les sortilèges* (The child and the sorcerers). Opera.
Wagner, Richard (1813–1883)
"Magic Fire Music" from *Die Walküre.* Orchestral work.


## MARIONETTES and PUPPETS — see also Dolls

Casella, Alfredo (1883–1947)
*Pupazzetti: Five Pieces for Marionettes.* Opus 27. Piano duet

Falla, Manuel de (1876–1946)
  *El Retablo de Maese Pedro* (Master Peter's puppet show). Opera.
Gounod, Charles (1818–1893)
  *Funeral March of a Marionette*. Orchestral work.
Stravinsky, Igor (1882–1971)
  *Petrushka*. Ballet

## MARKETPLACE

Ketelbey, Albert (1875–1959)
  *In a Persian Market*. Orchestral work.

Mussorgsky, Modest (1839–1881)
  "The Market Place at Limoges" from *Pictures at an Exhibition*. Piano;
  orchestral work.
Piston, Walter (1894–1976)
  "Siesta Hour in the Marketplace and Entrance of the Vendors" from
  *The Incredible Flutist*. Ballet.

## MARRIAGE — see Wedding

## MEXICO

Chávez, Carlos (1899–1978)
  *Cantos de México*. Mexican orchestra.
  *Cantos mexicanos*. Piano.
  *Sinfonía India*. Orchestral work.
  *Tocatta*. Percussion.
  *Xochipili–Macuilxochitl*. Mexican orchestra.
Copland, Aaron (1900–
  *El Salón México*. Orchestral work.
Purcell, Henry (1659–1695)
  *The Indian Queen*. Opera.
Revueltas, Silvestre (1899–1940)
  *Caminos* (Roads). Orchestral work.
  *Colorines* (Mexican tree). Orchestral work.
  *Cuauhnahuac* (Cuernavaca). Orchestral work.
  *Esquinas* (Corners). Orchestral work.
  *Janitzio*. Orchestral work.
  *Ventanas* (Windows). Orchestral work.
Sessions, Roger (1896–1985)
  *Montezuma*. Opera.

MILITARY — see also Soldiers, War, Weapons

Chopin, Frederic (1810–1849)
  Polanaise in A major *Military*. Opus 40, No. 1. Piano.
Haydn, Franz Joseph (1732–1809)
  Symphony No. 100 in G major *Military*.
Schubert, Franz (1797–1828)
  *Marches Militaires*. Nos. 1–3. Opus 51. Piano duet.
Suppé, Franz von (1819–1895)
  *Leichte Kavallerie* (Light cavalry). Orchestral work.
Zádor, Eugene (1894–1977)
  "Scherzo militaire" from *Children's Symphony*.


MOON — see also Sun, Universe

Beethoven, Ludwig van (1770–1827)
  Sonata No. 14 in C–sharp minor *Moonlight*. Opus 27, No. 2. Piano.
Britten, Benjamin (1913–1976)
  "Moonlight" from *Four Sea Interludes* from *Peter Grimes*. Opus 33a.
    Orchestral work.
Debussy, Claude (1862–1918)
  "Clair de lune" (Moonlight) from *Suite bergamasque*. Piano.
  "Et la lune descend sur le temple" (And the moon descends on the
    temple) from *Images II*. Piano.
  "Le Terrasse des audiences du clair de lune" (People on a terrace at
    moonlight) from *Préludes II*. Piano.
Ketelbey, Albert (1875–1959)
  *In the Moonlight*. Orchestral work.
MacDowell, Edward (1860–1908)
  "Clair de lune" (Moonlight) from *Les Orientales*. Opus 37. Piano.
  *Moon Pictures*. Opus 21. Piano duet. Five movements:
    (1) "The Hindoo Maiden" (2) "Stork's Story" (3) "In Tyrol"
    (4) "The Swan" (5) "Visit of the Bear."
  "Moonshine" from *Four Little Poems*. Opus 32. Piano.
  "To the Moonlight" from *Six Idyls after Goethe*. Opus 28. Piano.
Prokofiev, Sergei (1891–1953)
  "Moonlit Meadows" from *Summer Day*. Opus 65b. Orchestral work.


MORNING — see also Afternoon, Day, Evening, Night, Noon,
              Sunrise, Sunset

Britten, Benjamin (1913–1976)
  "Early Morning Bathe" from *Holiday Diary*. Opus 5. Piano.

"Sunday Morning" from *Four Sea Interludes* from *Peter Grimes*. Orchestral work.

Copland, Aaron (1900–
"Morning on the Ranch" from *The Red Pony*. Orchestral work.

Debussy, Claude (1862–1918)
"Le Matin d'un jour de fête" (Morning of a festival day) from *Iberia*. Orchestral work.
"Pour remercier la pluie au matin" (To remember the morning rain) from *Six Epigraphes antiques* (Six ancient inscriptions). Piano duet.

Falla, Manuel de (1876–1946)
"Morning Chimes" from *El Amor brujo* (Love, the magician). Ballet.

Grieg, Edvard (1843–1907)
"Morning Mood" from *Peer Gynt*. Suite No. 1. Opus 46. Orchestral work.

Haydn, Franz Joseph (1732–1809)
Symphony No. 6 in D major *Le Matin* (The morning).

Prokofiev, Sergei (1891–1953)
"Morning" from *Summer Day*. Opus 65b. Orchestral work.
"The Morning Dance" and "Morning Serenade" from *Romeo and Juliet*. Opus 101. Orchestral work.

Ravel, Maurice (1875–1937)
"Alborada del gracioso" (Morning serenade) from *Miroirs*. Piano.

Respighi, Ottorino (1879–1936)
"La Fontana del Tritone al mattino" (The fountain at Triton in the morning) from *Fontane di Roma* (Fountains of Rome). Orchestral work.

Siegmeister, Elie (1909–
"Morning in the Hills" from *Ozark Set*. Orchestral work.

Strauss, Johann Jr. (1825–1899)
*Morgenblätter* (Morning journals). Opus 279. Waltz.


MOUNTAINS — see also Hills

Bax, Arnold (1883–1953)
*Christmas Eve on the Mountains*. Orchestral work.

Berlioz, Hector (1803–1869)
"In the Mountains" from *Harold en Italie* (Harold in Italy). Opus 16. Viola and orchestra.

Berwald, Franz (1796–1868)
*Erinnerung an die Norwegischen Alpen* (Memories of the Norwegian Alps). Orchestral work.

Franck, César (1822–1890)
*Ce qu' on entend sur la montagne* (What one hears on the mountain). Orchestral work.

Grieg, Edvard (1843–1907)
*Evening in the Mountains*. Opus 68. Orchestral work.

"In the Hall of the Mountain King" from *Peer Gynt*. Suite No. 1.
Opus 46. Orchestral work.
Hill, Alfred (1870–1960)
*The Sacred Mountain*. Orchestral work.
Hovhaness, Alan (1911–
*Farewell to the Mountains*. Piano.
*Mountains and Rivers Without End*. Opus 225. Chamber music.
Symphony No. 2 *Mysterious Mountain*. Opus 132.
Indy, Vincent d' (1851–1931)
*Jour d'été à la montagne* (Summer day on the mountain). Opus 61.
Orchestral work. Three movements: (1) "L'Aube" (Dawn)
(2) "Le Jour" (Day) (3) "Le Soir" (Evening).
*Poème des montagnes* (Poem of the mountains). Opus 15. Piano.
Three movements: (1) "Chant des bruyères" (Song of the heath)
(2) "Brouillard" (Fog) (3) "Amour" (Love).
*Symphonie sur un chant montagnard français* (Symphony on a
French mountain song). Opus 25. Piano and orchestra.
Ippolitov–Ivanov, Mikhail (1859–1965)
"In the Mountain Pass" from *Caucasian Sketches*. Opus 10.
Orchestral work.
Ives, Charles (1874–1954)
*From the Steeples and the Mountains*. Orchestral work.
"The Call of the Mountains" from *String Quartet No. 2*.
Liszt, Franz (1811–1886)
*Ce qu'on entend sur la montagne* (What one hears on the mountain).
Orchestral work.
Mussorgsky, Modest (1839–1881)
*Night on Bald Mountain*. Orchestral work.
Piston, Walter (1894–1976)
"Mountains" from *Three New England Sketches*. Orchestral work.
Strauss, Richard (1864–1949)
*Eine Alpensinfonie* (An Alpine symphony). Opus 64.
Turina, Joaquín (1882–1949)
"Sacro Monte" (Sacred mountain) from *Danzas Gitanas*. Opus 55.
Piano.


MUSES — see also Greek Myths

Chadwick, George (1854–1931)
*Euterpe* (Muse of music). Orchestral work.
*Melpomene* (Muse of tragedy). Orchestral work.
*Thalia* (Muse of comedy). Orchestral work.
Saint–Saëns, Camille (1835–1921)
*La Muse et le poeta* (The muse and the poet). Opus 132. Violin,
cello and orchestra.
Stravinsky, Igor (1882–1971)
*Apollon Musagète* (Apollo, leader of the Muses). Ballet.

MUSIC and MUSICIANS — see also Greek Myths (Orpheus),
Musical Instruments

Bartók, Béla (1881–1945)
"Hommage à J.S.B." and "Hommage à R. Sch." from *Mikrokosmos*.
Book 3. Piano.
"With Drums and Pipes" from *Out of Doors*. Piano.
Ben–Haim, Paul (1897–1984)
*To the Chief Musician*. Orchestral work.
Chadwick, George (1854–1931)
*Euterpe* (Muse of music). Orchestral work.
Converse, Frederick (1871–1940)
*The Mystic Trumpeter*. Opus 19. Orchestral work.
Cowell, Henry (1897–1965)
Symphony No. 11 *Seven Rituals of Music*.
Debussy, Claude (1862–1918)
"Minstrels" from *Préludes I*. Piano.
Gottschalk, Louis Moreau (1829–1869)
*The Banjo*. Opus 15. Piano.
Hindemith, Paul (1895–1963)
*Der Schwanendreher* (The organ grinder). Viola and orchestra.
Hovhaness, Alan (1911–
*Fantasy for Piano*. Opus 16. (Inspired by Tumburu, the Indian God
of music).
Kuhnau, Johann (1660–1722)
"Saul Cured by David through Music" from *Biblical Sonatas*.
Harpsichord.
Moore, Douglas (1893–1969)
"Jenny Lind" from *The Pageant of P.T. Barnum*. Orchestral work.
Pfitzner, Hans (1869–1949)
*Palestrina*. Opera.
Piston, Walter (1894–1976)
*The Incredible Flutist*. Ballet. Thirteen movements:
(1) "Introduction" (2) "Siesta Hour in the Marketplace and Entrance
of the Vendors" (3) "Dance of the Vendors" (4) "Entrance of the
Customers" (5) "Tango of the Four Daughters" (6) "Arrival of the
Circus and Circus March" (7) "Solo of the Flutist"
(8) "Minuet — Dance of the Widow and Merchant" (9) "Spanish
Waltz" (10) "Eight O'Clock Strikes" (11) "Siciliano — Dance of
the Flutist and the Merchant's Daughter" (12) "Polka"
(13) "Finale."
Rachmaninoff, Sergei (1873–1943)
*Moments musicaux*. Opus 16. Piano.
Saint-Saëns, Camille (1835–1921)
"Pianists" from *Le Carnaval des animaux: fantaisie zoologique*
(Carnival of the animals: grand zoological fantasy). Orchestral
work.
Schubert, Franz (1797–1828)
*Moments musicaux*. Opus 94. Piano.

Schumann, Robert (1810–1856)
  "Chopin" and "Paganini" from *Carnaval*. Opus 9. Piano.
Shebalin, Vissarion (1902–1963)
  *Mozart and Salieri*. Incidental music.
Shostakovich, Dmitri (1906–1975)
  Symphony No. 5 (A Soviet artist's reply to just criticism). Opus 47.
Thomson, Virgil (1896–
  *Symphony on a Hymn Tune.*
Villa–Lobos, Heitor (1887–1959)
  *Rudepoema* (Savage poem — portrait of Artur Rubinstein). Piano.
Wagner, Richard (1813–1883)
  *Die Meistersinger von Nürnberg.* Opera.
Weinberger, Jaromir (1896–1967)
  *Schwanda der Dudelsackpfeifer* (Schwanda, the bagpiper). Opera.


MUSICAL INSTRUMENTS — see also Music and Musicians

Anderson, Leroy (1908–1975)
  *Bugler's Holiday.* Orchestral work.
Bartók, Béla (1881–1945)
  "Bagpipe" from *Mikrokosmos.* Book 5. Piano.
  "Duet for Pipes" from *Mikrokosmos.* Book 3. Piano.
Beethoven, Ludwig van (1770–1827)
  Sonata No. 29 in B–flat major *Hammerklavier.* Opus 106. Piano.
  Quartet in E–flat major *The Harp.* Opus 74. String quartet.
Bizet, Georges (1838–1875)
  "Trompette et tambour" (Trumpet and drum) from *Jeux d'enfants*
    (Children's games). Piano duet.
Britten, Benjamin (1913–1976)
  *Young Person's Guide to the Orchestra.* Opus 34. Narrator and
    orchestra.
Chopin, Frederic (1810–1849)
  Etude in A–flat major *Harp.* Opus 25, No. 1. Piano.
  Etude in C–sharp minor *Cello.* Opus 25, No. 7. Piano.
  Etude in G–flat major *Black Key.* Opus 10, No. 5. Piano.
Gottschalk, Louis Moreau (1829–1869)
  *Aeolian Harp.* Piano.
  *The Banjo.* Piano.
Haydn, Franz Joseph (1732–1809)
  Symphony No. 103 in E–flat major *Paukenwirbel* (Drum roll).
Messiaen, Olivier (1908–
  "Hallelujah on the Trumpet, Hallelujah on the Cymbal" from
    *L'Ascension* (The ascension). Orchestral work.
Mozart, Wolfgang Amadeus (1756–1791)
  *Die Zauberflöte* (The magic flute). K. 620. Opera.
  Quartet in D major *Cello.* K. 575. String quartet.

Reger, Max (1873–1916)
"Der Geigende Eremit" (The hermit with the violin) from *Vier Tondichtungen nach Arnold Böcklin* (Four tone poems after Arnold Böcklin). Opus 128. Orchestral work.

Stravinsky, Igor (1882–1971)
"Soldier's Violin" from *L'Histoire du soldat* (The soldier's tale). Narrator and ballet.

Tchaikovsky, Peter Ilyich (1840–1893)
"Dance of the Flutes" from *Nutcracker Suite*. Opus 71a. Ballet.

Thomson, Virgil (1896–
"Bugles and Birds (A portait of Pablo Picasso)" from *Portraits*. Album 1. Piano.


MYTHS — see also Folk Tales, Greek Myths

Glazunov, Alexander (1865–1936)
*A Karelian Legend*. Opus 98. Orchestral work.

Klami, Uuno (1900–1961)
*Kalevala Suite*. Opus 23. Orchestral work.
*Karelian Rhapsody*. Opus 15. Orchestral work.
*Lemminkäinen*. Opus 24. Orchestral work.

Madetoja, Leevi (1887–1947)
*Kullervo*. Opus 15. Orchestral work.

Prokofiev, Sergei (1891–1953)
*Scythian Suite*. Opus 20. Orchestral work.

Sibelius, Jean (1865–1957)
*Four Legends*. Opus 22. Orchestral work. Four movements: (1) "Lemminkäinen and the Maidens" (2) "Lemminkäinen in Tuonela" (3) "The Swan of Tuonela" (4) "Lemminkäinen's Homeward Journey."
*Karelia Suite*. Opus 11. Orchestral work.

Wagner, Richard (1813–1883)
*Der Ring von des Nibelungen* (Ring of the Nibelungs). Opus 78. Music drama. Four operas: (1) "Das Rheingold" (The Rhinegold) (2) "Die Walküre" (The Valkyries) (3) "Siegfried" (4) "Götterdämmerung" (Twilight of the Gods).

# N

NATURE — see also Clouds, Countryside, Flowers, Forest, Hills, Lakes, Leaves, Mountains, Pastoral, Prairie, Ocean, Rain, Rivers, Snow, Storm, Trees, Water, Weather, Wind, Will–o'–the–Wisp

Bartók, Béla (1881–1945)
  *Out of Doors*. Piano. Five movements: (1) "With Drums and Pipes" (2) "Barcarolla" (3) "Musettes" (4) "Musiques Nocturnes" (5) "The Chase."
Bax, Arnold (1883–1953)
  *Nympholept*. Orchestral work.
Dvořák, Antonín (1841–1904)
  *In Nature's Realm*. Opus 91. Orchestral work.
Grofé, Ferde (1892–1972)
  *Grand Canyon Suite*. Five movements: (1) "Sunrise" (2) "The Painted Desert" (3) "On the Trail" (4) "Sunset" (5) "Cloudburst."
Indy, Vincent d' (1851–1931)
  "Chant des bruyères" (Song of the heath) from *Poème des montagnes* (Poem of the mountains). Opus 15. Piano.
Janáček, Leos (1854–1928)
  *Idyll*. String orchestra.
Malipiero, Gian Francesco (1882–1973)
  *Impressioni dal vero* (Impressions from nature). Orchestral work. Three movements: (1) "Il Capinero" (The blackcap) (2) "Il Picchio" (The woodpecker) (3) "Il Chiù" (The owl).

NIGHT — see also Afternoon, Day, Evening, Morning, Noon, Sunrise, Sunset

Bloch, Ernest (1880–1959)
  *Exotic Night*. Violin and piano.
  *In the Night*. Piano.
  *Night*. String quartet.
Britten, Benjamin (1913–1976)
  "Night" from *Holiday Diary*. Opus 5. Piano.
Copland, Aaron (1900–
  "Card Game at Night" from *Billy the Kid*. Ballet.
  "Night Thoughts" from *Music for a Great City*. Orchestral work.
  "Saturday Night Waltz" from *Rodeo*. Ballet.

Debussy, Claude (1862–1918)
"Les Parfums de la nuit" (Perfumes of the night) from *Iberia*.
Orchestral work.
"Les Sons et les parfums tournent dans l'air du soir" (Sounds and
perfumes in the evening air) from *Préludes I*. Piano.
"Pour que la nuit soit propice" (That night may be propitious) from
*Six Epigraphes antiques* (Six ancient inscriptions). Piano duet.
"Soirée dans Grenade" (Evening in Granada) from *Estampes*
(Engravings). Piano.
Delius, Frederick (1862–1934)
"Summer Night on the River" from *Two Pieces for Small Orchestra*.
Elgar, Edward (1857–1934)
"The Queen's Tower at Night" from *King Arthur Suite*. Orchestral
work.
Falla, Manuel de (1876–1946)
*Noches en los jardines de España* (Nights in the gardens of Spain).
Piano and orchestra. Three movements: (1) "En el Generalife" (At
the Generalife) (2) "Danza Lejana" (A far–off dance) (3) "En los
jardines de la Sierra de Córdoba" (In the gardens of the Sierra of
Cordoba).
Foote, Arthur (1853–1937)
*A Night Piece*. Flute and string quartet.
Glinka, Mikhail (1804–1857)
*Summer Night in Madrid*. Orchestral work.
Griffes, Charles Tomlinson (1884–1920)
"Nightfall" from *Four Roman Sketches*. Opus 7. Piano; orchestral
work.
Indy, Vincent d' (1851–1931)
"Le Soir" (Night) from *Jour d'été à la montagne* (Summer day on the
mountain). Opus 61. Piano and orchestra.
MacDowell, Edward (1860–1908)
"Night at Sea" from *Three Poems*. Opus 20. Piano duet.
Mendelssohn, Felix (1809–1847)
*A Midsummer Night's Dream*. Opus 21. Orchestral work.
Mozart, Wolfgang Amadeus (1756–1791)
*Eine kleine Nachtmusik* (A little night music). K. 525. String
orchestra.
Mussorgsky, Modest (1839–1881)
*Night on Bald Mountain*. Orchestral work.
Prokofiev, Sergei (1891–1953)
*Egyptian Night*. Opus 61. Orchestral work.
Rabaud, Henri (1873–1949)
*La Procession nocturne* (The nocturnal procession). Opus 6.
Orchestral work.
Ravel, Maurice (1875–1937)
*Gaspard de la nuit* (Scents of the night). Piano. Three movements:
(1) "Ondine" (2) "Le Gibet" (The gallows) (3) "Scarbo."
"Prélude à la nuit" (Prelude of the night) from *Rapsodie espagnole*
(Spanish rhapsody). Orchestral work.

Respighi, Ottorino (1879–1936)
  "Notte tropicale" (Tropical night) from *Impressioni brasiliane* (Brazilian impressions). Orchestral work.
Schönberg, Arnold (1874–1951)
  *Verklärte Nacht* (Transfigured night). Opus 4. String sextet; string orchestra.
Schumann, Robert (1810–1856)
  "In der Nacht" (By night) from *Fantasiestücke*. Opus 12. Piano.
  *Nachtstücke* (Night pieces). Opus 23. Piano.
Sibelius, Jean (1865–1957)
  *Night Ride and Sunrise*. Opus 55. Orchestral work.
Siegmeister, Elie (1909–
  "Saturday Night" from *Ozark Set*. Orchestral work.
Tchaikovsky, Peter Ilyich (1840–1893)
  "May: Bright Nights" from *The Seasons*. Opus 37b. Piano.


NOON — see also Afternoon, Day, Evening, Morning, Night, Sunrise, Sunset

Debussy, Claude (1862–1918)
  "De l'aube à midi sur la mer" (From dawn to noon on the sea) from *La Mer* (The sea). Orchestral work.
Dvořák, Antonín (1841–1904)
  *The Noonday Witch*. Opus 108. Orchestral work.
Haydn, Franz Joseph (1732–1809)
  Symphony No. 7 in C major *Le Midi* (Midday).
Respighi, Ottorino (1879–1936)
  "La Fontana di Trevi al meriggio" (The fountain of Trevi at midday) from *Fontane di Roma* (Fountains of Rome). Orchestral work.
Thomson, Virgil (1896–
  *Wheat Fields at Noon*. Orchestral work.


NORWAY

Berwald, Franz (1796–1868)
  *Erinnerung an die Norwegischen Alpen* (Memories of the Norwegian Alps). Orchestral work.
Delius, Frederick (1862–1934)
  *Eventyr* (Once upon a time). Orchestral work.
Grieg, Edvard (1843–1907)
  *Lyric Suite*. Opus 54. Orchestral work. Four movements:
    (1) "Shepherd's Lad" (2) "Norwegian Rustic Dance"
    (3) "Nocturne" (4) "March of the Dwarfs."
  *Norwegian Dances and Songs*. Opus 17. Piano.

*Peer Gynt.* Suite No. 1. Opus 46. Orchestral work.
Four movements: (1) "Morning" (2) "Åse's Death"
(3) "Anitra's Dance" (4) "In the Hall of the Mountain King."
*Peer Gynt.* Suite No. 2. Opus 55. Orchestral work.
Four movements: (1) "The Abduction and Ingrid's Lament"
(2) "Arab Dance" (3) "Peer Gynt's Homecoming"
(4) "Solveig's Song."
*Two Norwegian Melodies.* Opus 63. Orchestral work.
Two movements: (1) "In the Style of a Folksong"
(2) "Cowkeeper's Tune and Peasant Dance."
Lalo, Edouard (1823–1892)
*Rhapsodie norvégienne* (Norwegian rhapsody). Orchestral work.
MacDowell, Edward (1860–1908)
Sonata No. 3 *Norse.* Opus 57. Piano.
Stravinsky, Igor (1882–1971)
*Four Norwegian Moods.* Orchestral work. Four movements:
(1) "Intrada" (2) "Song" (3) "Wedding Dance" (4) "Cortège."
Svendsen, Johan Severin (1840–1911)
*Norwegian Artists' Carnival.* Opus 16. Orchestral work.


NYMPHS — see Fairy World


# O


OCCUPATIONS — see also Farm and Farmers, Shepherd and
Shepherdess

Berlioz, Hector (1803–1869)
*Le Corsaire* (The pirate). Opus 21. Orchestral work.
Carpenter, John Alden (1876–1951)
"The Policeman" from *Adventures in a Perambulator.* Orchestral work.
Copland, Aaron (1900–
*Billy the Kid.* Ballet.
*Fanfare for the Common Man.* Orchestral work.
Couperin, François (1631–1701)
*Les Moissonneurs* (The harvesters). Ordre 6, No. 1. Harpsichord.
Handel, George Frideric (1685–1759)
"The Harmonious Blacksmith" from Suite No. 5 in E major.
Harpsichord.
Medtner, Nikolai (1880–1951)
*Three Hymns in Praise of Toil.* Opus 49. Piano. Three movements:
(1) "Before Labour" (2) "At the Anvil" (3) "After Labour."

Mozart, Wolfgang Amadeus (1756–1791)
*Der Schauspieldirektor* (The impresario). K. 486. Opera.
Pergolesi, Giovanni Battista (1710–1736)
*La Serva padrona*. Opera.
Piston, Walter (1894–1976)
"Dance of the Vendors" from *The Incredible Flutist*. Ballet.
Prokofiev, Sergei (1891–1953)
"The Nurse" from *Romeo and Juliet*. Opus 101. Orchestral work.
Rossini, Gioacchino (1792–1868)
*Il Barbiere di Siviglia* (The barber of Seville). Opera.
Scott, Cyril (1879–1970)
*The Alchemist*. Opera.
Siegmeister, Elie (1909–
"Bullwhacker's Dance" from *Prairie Legend*. Orchestral work.
Strauss, Richard (1864–1949)
"The Fencing Master" and "Entrance and Dance of the Tailors" from
*La Bourgeois gentilhomme*. Opus 66.
Tchaikovsky, Peter Ilyich (1840–1893)
"July: Reaper's Song" from *The Seasons*. Opus 37b. Piano.
Turina, Joaquín (1882–1949)
*L'Oración del torero* (The bullfighter's prayer). Opus 34. String
quartet.
"Los pescadores in Bajo de Guía" (The fisherman in Bajo de Guía)
from *Sanlúcar del Barrameda*. Opus 24. Piano.
Wagner, Richard (1813–1883)
"Dance of the Apprentices" from *Die Meistersinger von Nürnberg*
(The master singer from Nürnberg). Orchestral work.


OCEAN — see also Water, Waves

Bax, Arnold (1883–1953)
*The Garden of Fand*. Orchestral work.
Bloch, Ernest (1880–1959)
*Poems of the Sea*. Piano. Three movements: (1) "Waves"
(2) "Chanty" (3) "At Sea."
Britten, Benjamin (1913–1976)
"Four Sea Interludes" from *Peter Grimes*. Orchestral work.
Four movements: (1) "Dawn" (2) "Sunday Morning"
(3) "Moonlight" (4) "The Storm."
Carpenter, John Alden (1876–1951)
*Sea Drift*. Orchestral work.
Debussy, Claude (1862–1918)
*La Mer* (The sea). Orchestral work. Three movements:
(1) "De l'aube à midi sur la mer" (From dawn to noon on the sea)
(2) "Jeux de vagues" (Play of the waves) (3) "Dialogue du vent et
de la mer" (Dialogue of the the wind and the sea).

Glazunov, Alexander (1865–1936)
*The Sea.* Opus 28. Orchestral work.
MacDowell, Edward (1860–1908)
"Night at Sea" from *Three Poems.* Opus 20. Piano duet.
"Sea Pieces." Opus 55. Piano. Eight movements: (1) "To the Sea"
(2) "From a Wandering Iceberg" (3) "A.D. 1620" (4) "Starlight"
(5) "Song" (6) "From the Depths" (7) "Nautilus"
(8) "In Mid–Ocean."
Mendelssohn, Felix (1809–1847)
*Meeresstille und glückliche Fahrt* (Calm sea and prosperous voyage).
Opus 27. Orchestral work.
Rachmaninoff, Sergei (1873–1943)
"The Sea and Seagulls" from *Etudes–Tableaux.* Opus 39, No. 2.
Piano.
Ravel, Maurice (1875–1937)
"Une Barque sur l'océan" (A Boat on the ocean) from *Miroirs*
(Mirrors). Piano.
Rimsky–Korsakov, Nikolai (1844–1908)
"The Sea and Sinbad's Ship" from *Scheherazade.* Opus 35.
Orchestral work.
Rogowski, Ludomir (1881–1954)
"Sea–crossing of Merlin" from *A Celtic Legend.* Orchestral work.
Rubinstein, Anton (1829–1894)
Symphony No. 2 in C major *Ocean.* Opus 42.
Sibelius, Jean (1865–1957)
"By the Sea" from *Pelléas et Mélisande.* Opus 46. Orchestral work.
*The Oceanides.* Opus 73. Orchestral work.
Smetana, Bedrich (1824–1884)
*On the Seashore.* Piano.
Vaughan Williams, Ralph (1872–1958)
*Sea Songs.* Brass band.


ORIENTAL — see also China, Japan, Persia

Bartók, Béla (1881–1945)
"In Oriental Style" from *Mikrokosmos.* Book 2. Piano.
Cui, César (1835–1918)
"Orientale" from *Kaleidoscope.* Opus 50. Violin and piano.
Glazunov, Alexander (1865–1936)
*Oriental Rhapsody.* Opus 29. Orchestral work.
MacDowell, Edward (1860–1908)
*Les Orientales.* Opus 37. Piano. Three movements:
(1) "Clair de lune" (Moonlight) (2) "Dans le hamac" (In the
hammock) (3) "Danse andalouse" (Andalusian dance).
Rachmaninoff, Sergei (1873–1943)
"Oriental March" from *Etudes–Tableaux.* Opus 39, No. 9. Piano.

# P

PARADE — see also Carnival, Circus, Festivals

Moore, Douglas (1893–1969)
"Circus Parade" from *The Pageant of P.T. Barnum.* Orchestral work.
Satie, Erik (1866–1925)
*Parade.* Ballet.
Turina, Joaquín (1882–1949)
*La Procesión del Rocío* (The procession of the dew). Opus 9.
Orchestral work.

PARK

Dello Joio, Norman (1913–
"The Park" from *New York Profiles.* Orchestral work.
Sibelius, Jean (1865–1957)
"A Fountain in the Park" from *Pelléas et Mélisande.* Opus 46.
Orchestral work.

PASTORAL — see also Nature

Beethoven, Ludwig van (1770–1827)
Sonata No. 15 in D major *Pastoral.* Opus 28. Piano.
Quartet in E–flat major *Pastoral.* Opus 127. String quartet.
Symphony No. 6 in F major *Pastoral.* Opus 68. Five movements:
(1) "The Awakening of Joyful Feelings upon Arrival in the
Country" (2) "Scene by the Brook" (3) "Village Festival"
(4) "The Storm" (5) "The Shepherd's Song."
Chabrier, Emmanuel (1841–1894)
*Suite pastorale.* Orchestral work.
Honegger, Arthur (1892–1955)
*Pastorale d'été* (Summer pastoral). Orchestral work.
Ireland, John (1879–1962)
*Concertino pastorale.* String orchestra.
Larsson, Lars–Erik (1908–
*Pastoral Suite.* Opus 19. Orchestral work.
Liszt, Franz (1811–1886)
"Pastorale" and "Eglogue" (Pastoral poem) from *Années de
pèlerinage: Première année: Suisse* (Years of pilgrimage: first
year: Switzerland).

Mason, Daniel Gregory (1873–1953)
*Pastorale.* Opus 8. Violin, clarinet and piano.
Vaughan Williams, Ralph (1872–1958)
Symphony No. 3 *Pastoral.*


# PEACE

Hanson, Howard (1896–1981)
"Peace" from *Four Poems.* Opus 9. Piano.
Harris, Roy (1898–1979)
"Praise and Thanksgiving for Peace" from Symphony No. 10 *Abraham Lincoln.*
Holst, Gustav (1874–1934)
"Venus, the Bringer of Peace" from *The Planets.* Opus 32. Orchestral work.
Prokofiev, Sergei (1891–1953)
*War and Peace.* Opus 91. Opera.
Strauss, Richard (1864–1949)
"The Hero's Mission of Peace" from *Ein Heldenleben* (A hero's life). Opus 40. Orchestral work.


# PEASANTS

Schumann, Robert (1810–1856)
"Fröhlicher Landmann" (Merry peasant) from *Album für die Jugend* (Album for the young). Opus 68. Piano.
Suppé, Franz von (1819–1895)
*The Poet and the Peasant.* Orchestral work.


# PERSIA

Handel, George Frideric (1685–1759)
*Serse* (Xerxes). Opera.
Ketelbey, Albert (1875–1959)
*In a Persian Market.* Orchestral work.
Rameau, Jean–Philippe (1683–1764)
*Zoroastre.* Opera.
Sibelius, Jean (1865–1957)
*Belshazzar's Feast.* Opus 51. Orchestral work.
Strauss, Richard (1864–1949)
*Also sprach Zarathustra* (Thus spoke Zarathustra). Opus 30. Orchestral work.

## PHILOSOPHIES

Bernstein, Leonard (1918–
*The Age of Anxiety*. Piano and orchestra. Two parts:
Part I: The Prologue; The Seven Ages; The Seven Stages.
Part II: The Dirge; The Masque; The Epilogue.
Bloch, Ernest (1880–1959)
*A Voice in the Wilderness*. Orchestral work.
Carpenter, John Alden (1876–1951)
*The Seven Ages*. Orchestral work.
Chávez, Carlos (1899–1978)
*H.P.* (Horsepower). Symphony; ballet.
Cowell, Henry (1897–1965)
Symphony No. 11 *Seven Rituals of Music*.
Haydn, Franz Joseph (1732–1809)
Symphony No. 22 in E–flat major *The Philosopher*.
Hindemith, Paul (1895–1963)
*Die Harmonie der Welt* (The harmony of the world). Opera; orchestral
work. Three movements: (1) "Musica Instrumentalis" (2) "Musica
Humana" (3) "Musica Mundana." (Inspired by Johannes Kepler.)
Hovhaness, Alan (1911–
*Floating World – Ukiyo*. Opus 209. Orchestral work.
Ives, Charles (1874–1954)
"Emerson" and "Thoreau" from Sonata No. 2 *Concord*. Piano.
Liszt, Franz (1811–1886)
*Les Préludes*. Orchestral work.
Martinu, Bohuslav (1890–1959)
*Parables*. Orchestral work. Three movements: (1) "The Parable of
Sculpture" (2) "The Parable of a Garden" (3) "The Parable of a
Labyrinth."
Messiaen, Olivier (1908–
*Trois petits liturgies de la présence divine* (Three little liturgies of the
Divine Presence). Orchestral work.
*Visions de l'amen*. Two pianos. Eight movements: (1) "Amen of the
Creation" (2) "Amen of the Stars, of the Planet Saturn"
(3) "Amen of the Agony of Jesus" (4) "Amen of Desire"
(5) "Amen of the Angels, of the Saints, of the Song of the Birds"
(6) "Amen of Judgment" (7) "Amen of Consummation."
Nielsen, Carl (1865–1931)
Symphony No. 4 *The Inextinguishable*. Opus 29. Orchestral work.
Scriabin, Alexander (1872–1915)
*Poem of Ecstasy*. Opus 54. Orchestral work.
Symphony No. 3 in C major *The Divine Poem*. Opus 43.
Strauss, Richard (1864–1949)
*Also sprach Zarathustra* (Thus spoke Zarathustra). Opus 30.
Orchestral work.

Subotnick, Morton (1933–
  *The Double Life of Amphibians.* Orchestral work. Three movements:
  (1) "Ascent into Air" (2) "The Last Dream of the Beast"
  (3) "Angels (A Fluttering of Wings)."

# PILGRIMS

Berlioz, Hector (1803–1869)
  "March and Evening of the Pilgrims" from *Harold en Italie* (Harold in
  Italy). Opus 16. Viola and orchestra.
Bloch, Ernest (1880–1959)
  "1620. The Soil – the Indians – the Mayflower – the Landing
  Pilgrims" from *America: An Epic Rhapsody.* Orchestral work.
Glière, Reinhold (1875–1956)
  "Wandering Pilgrims: Ilia Mourometz and Sviatogar" from Symphony
  No. 3 in B minor *Ilia Mourometz.* Opus 42. Orchestral work.
Mendelssohn, Felix (1809–1847)
  "Pilgrim's March" from Symphony No. 4 in A major *Italian.* Opus 90.

# POETRY and POETS

Gottschalk, Louis Moreau (1829–1869)
  *The Dying Poet.* Piano.
Malipiero, Gian Francesco (1882–1973)
  *Rispetti and Strambottio.* String quartet.
Saint–Saëns, Camille (1835–1921)
  *La Muse et la poète* (The muse and the poet). Opus 132. Violin, cello
  and orchestra.
Schumann, Robert (1810–1856)
  "Der Dichter spricht" (The poet speaks) from *Kinderscenen* (Scenes of
  childhood). Opus 15. Piano.
Suppé, Franz von (1819–1895)
  *The Poet and the Peasant.* Orchestral work.

# POLAND — see also Cities (Polish)

Chopin, Frederic (1810–1849)
  *Mazurkas* (61). Piano.
  *Polonaises* (16). Piano.
Elgar, Edward (1857–1934)
  *Polonia.* Opus 76. Orchestral work.

Paderewski, Ignace Jan (1860–1941)
  *Polish Dances*. Opus 9. Piano.
  *Polish Fantasy on Original Themes for Piano*. Opus 19. Piano and
    orchestra.
Tchaikovsky, Peter Ilyich (1840–1893)
  Symphony No. 3 in D major *Polish*. Opus 29.
Wagner, Richard (1813–1883)
  *Polonia*. Orchestral work.


# PRAIRIE

Antheil, George (1900–1959)
  *Over the Plains*. Orchestral work.
Copland, Aaron (1900–
  *Saga of the Prairie*. Orchestral work.
  "The Open Prairie" and "The Open Prairie Again" from *Billy the Kid*.
    Ballet.
Creston, Paul (1906–1985)
  *Frontiers*. Opus 34. Orchestral work.
Dello Joio, Norman (1913–
  *Prairie*. Ballet.
Siegmeister, Elie (1909–
  *Prairie Legend*. Orchestral work. Three movements:
    (1) "Bullwhacker's Dance"  (2) "Harvest Evening"  (3) "Country
    Fair."
Sowerby, Leo (1895–1968)
  *Prairie*. Orchestral work.
Thomson, Virgil (1896–
  *The Plow that Broke the Plains*. Orchestral work. Six movements:
    (1) "Prelude"  (2) "Pastorale" (Grass)  (3) "Cattle"  (4) "Blues"
    (Speculation)  (5) "Drought"  (6) "Devastation."


PUPPETS — see Marionettes and Puppets

# Q

QUEENS — see Royalty

## QUESTION

Beethoven, Ludwig van (1770–1827)
    Quartet in F major *Müss es sein? Es müss sein!* (Must it be?
    It must be!). Opus 135. String quartet.
Haydn, Franz Joseph (1732–1809)
    Quartet No. 41 in G major *How do you do?* Opus 33, No. 5. String
    quartet.
Ives, Charles (1874–1954)
    *The Unanswered Question.* Orchestral work.
Schumann, Robert (1810–1856)
    "Warum?" (Why?) from *Fantasiestücke.* Opus 12.
    Piano.

# R

RAIN — see also Rainbow, Water

Brahms, Johannes (1833–1897)
    Sonata in G major *Rain Sonata.* Opus 78. Violin and piano.
Chopin, Frederic (1810–1849)
    Prelude No. 15 in D–flat major *Raindrop.* Opus 28. Piano.
Debussy, Claude (1862–1918)
    "Jardins sous la pluie" (Gardens in the rain) from *Estampes*
        (Engravings). Piano.
    "Pour remercier la pluie au matin" (To remember the morning rain)
        from *Six Epigraphes antiques* (Six ancient inscriptions). Piano
        duet.
Rieti, Vittorio (1898–
    "The Flood" from *L'Arca di Noé* (Noah's Ark). Orchestral work.

RAINBOW — see also Rain

Messiaen, Olivier (1908–
"Fouillis d'arcs–en–ciel, pour l'ange qui annonce la fin du temps"
(Cluster of rainbows, for the angel who announces the end of time)
from *Quatuor pour la fin du temps* (Quartet for the end of time).
Clarinet, violin, cello, piano.
Rieti, Vittorio (1898–
"The Rainbow" from *L'Arca di Noé* (Noah's Ark). Orchestral work.


RELIGIOUS FIGURES — see also Bible, Christ

Bach, Johann Sebastian (1685–1750)
Fugue No. 9 in E major "Saints in Glory" from *Well–Tempered Clavier*. Book 2. Piano, harpsichord.
Prelude and Fugue in E–flat major *St. Anne's*. Organ.
Bliss, Arthur (1891–1975)
"Ceremony of the Red Bishops" from *Checkmate*. Ballet.
Bloch, Ernest (1880–1959)
*Baal Shem: Three Pictures of Chassidic Life*. Violin and piano.
Three movements: (1) "Yidui" (Contrition) (2) "Nigun" (Improvisation) (3) "Simchas Torah" (Rejoicing).
Castelnuovo–Tedesco, Mario (1895–1968)
Concerto No. 2 *The Prophets*. Violin and orchestra.
Three movements: (1) "Isaiah" (2) "Jeremiah" (3) "Elijah."
Hanson, Howard (1896–1981)
*Pan and the Priest*. Orchestral work.
Harris, Roy (1898–1979)
Symphony No. 8 *San Francisco*.
Hindemith, Paul (1895–1963)
*Nobilissima visione*. Ballet. (Inspired by St. Francis.)
"Temptation of St. Anthony" from *Mathis der Maler* (Matthias the painter). Opera; orchestral work.
Hovhaness, Alan (1911–
*Prayer of Saint Gregory*. Trumpet and string orchestra.
Liszt, Franz (1811–1886)
"St. François d'Assise prédicant aux oiseaux" (St. Francis of Assisi's sermon to the birds) from *Légendes*. Piano.
"St. François de Paule marchant sur les flots" (St. Francis of Paola walking on the waves) from *Légendes*. Piano.
Mendelssohn, Felix (1809–1847)
"War March of the Priests" from *Athalia*. Opus 74. Orchestral work.
Messiaen, Olivier (1908–
*Trois petits liturgies de la Présence Divine* (Three little liturgies of the Divine Presence). Orchestral work.

Prokofiev, Sergei (1891–1953)
"Friar Laurence" from *Romeo and Juliet*. Opus 64–ter. Orchestral work.
Rameau, Jean–Philippe (1683–1764)
*Zoroastre*. Opera.
Respighi, Ottorino (1879–1936)
"Mattutino di Santa Chiara" (The Matin of Saint Claire) and "San Gregorio Magno" (St. Gregory the Great) from *Vetrate di chiesa* (Church windows). Orchestral work.
Schumann, Robert (1810–1856)
"Vogel als Prophet" (Bird as prophet) from *Waldscenen* (Forest scenes). Opus 82, No. 7. Piano.
Strauss, Richard (1864–1949)
*Also sprach Zarathustra* (Thus spoke Zarathustra). Opus 30. Orchestral work.

REVOLUTION — see also War

Chopin, Frederic (1810–1849)
Étude No. 12 in C minor *Revolutionary*. Opus 10, No. 12. Piano.
Polonaise in E–flat minor *Revolt*. Opus 26, No. 2. Piano.
Shostakovich, Dmitri (1906–1975)
Symphony No. 2 *October*. Opus 14.

RIVERS — see also Water

Beethoven, Ludwig van (1770–1827)
"Scene by the Brook" from Symphony No. 6 in F major *Pastorale*. Opus 68.
Delius, Frederick (1862–1934)
"Summer Night on The River" from *Two Pieces for Small Orchestra*.
Hovhaness, Alan (1911–
*Mountains and Rivers Without End*. Opus 225. Chamber music.
Ippolitov–Ivanov, Mikhail (1859–1965)
*On the Volga*. Opus 50. Orchestral work.
MacDowell, Edward (1860–1908)
"The Brook" from *Four Little Poems*. Opus 32. Piano.
McDonald, Harl (1899–1955)
*Saga of the Mississippi*. Orchestral work.
Schumann, Robert (1810–1856)
Symphony No. 3 in E–flat major *Rhenish*. Opus 97.
Smetana, Bedrich (1824–1884)
"Vltava" (The Moldau) from *Má Vlast* (My country). Orchestral work.

Strauss, Johann Jr. (1825–1899)
*An der schönen blauen Donau* (On the beautiful blue Danube).
Opus 314. Waltz.
Stravinsky, Igor (1882–1971)
*Song of the Haulers on the Volga*. Wind instruments.
Thomson, Virgil (1896–
*The River*. Orchestral work.
Wagner, Richard (1813–1883)
"Siegfried's Rhine Journey" from *Götterdämmerung* (Twilight of the Gods). Orchestral work.


ROYALTY — see also King Arthur Legends, Knights, Shakespeare

Beethoven, Ludwig van (1770–1827)
*König Stephan* (King Stephen). Opus 117. Incidental music.
Concerto No. 5 in E–flat major *Emperor*. Opus 73. Piano and orchestra.
Trio No. 6 in B–flat major *Archduke Trio*. Opus 97. Piano, violin and cello.
Bliss, Arthur (1891–1975)
"The Entry of the Black Queen" from *Checkmate*. Ballet.
Carpenter, John Alden (1876–1951)
*The Birthday of the Infanta*. Ballet. Three movements:
(1) "The Guest" (2) "The Infanta" (3) "The Games."
Castelnuovo–Tedesco, Mario (1895–1968)
*The Birthday of the Infanta*. Ballet. Seven movements: (1) "Fanfare"
(2) "Sarabande of the King of Spain" (3) "Pavane of the Infanta"
(4) "Ronde of Las Meninas" (5) "Minuet of the Rose" (6) "Dance of the Mirror" (7) "Epilogue."
Chabrier, Emmanuel (1841–1894)
*Le Roi malgré lui* (The king in spite of himself). Opera.
Chadwick, George (1854–1931)
*Cleopatra*. Orchestral work.
Donizetti, Gaetano (1797–1848)
*Anna Bolena*. Opera.
*Maria Stuarda*. Opera.
Grieg, Edvard (1843–1907)
"In the Hall of the Mountain King" from *Peer Gynt*. Suite No. 1.
Opus 46. Orchestral work.
Haydn, Franz Joseph (1732–1809)
Quartet No. 77 in C major *Emperor*. Opus 76, No. 3. String quartet.
Symphony No. 85 in B–flat major *La Reine* (The queen).
Humperdinck, Engelbert (1854–1921)
*Königskinder* (King's children). Opera.
Kodály, Zoltán (1882–1967)
"Entrance of the Emperor and his Court" from *Háry János*.
Orchestral work.

Monteverdi, Claudio (1567–1643)
*L'Incoronazione di Poppea* (The coronation of Poppea). Opera.

Mozart, Wolfgang Amadeus (1756–1791)
Concerto No. 26 in D major *Coronation*. K. 537. Piano and orchestra.
*Thamos, König in Aegypten* (Thamos, King of Egypt). K. 345. Incidental music.

Prokofiev, Sergei (1891–1953)
"Dance of King Dodon and the Queen of Shenakha" from *Le Coq d'or* (The golden cockerel). Orchestral work.

Purcell, Henry (1659–1695)
*The Indian Queen*. Opera.

Rameau, Jean–Philippe (1683–1764)
*La Princesse de Navarre* (The princess of Navarre). Opera.

Ravel, Maurice (1875–1937)
*Pavane pour une infante défunte* (Pavane for a dead princess). Orchestral work.

Rimsky–Korsakov, Nikolai (1844–1908)
"The Young Prince and the Princess" and "The Kalendar Prince" from *Scheherazade*. Opus 35. Orchestral work.

Rubinstein, Anton (1829–1894)
*Ivan the Terrible*. Opus 79. Orchestral work.

Saint–Saëns, Camille (1835–1921)
*Henry VIII*. Opera.

Sessions, Roger (1896–1985)
*Montezuma*. Opera.

Strauss, Johann Jr. (1825–1899)
*Kaiserwalzer* (Emperor). Opus 437. Waltz.

Taylor, Deems (1885–1966)
*The King's Henchman*. Opera.

Wagner, Richard (1813–1883)
*Kaisermarsch* (Emperor's march). Orchestral work.


# RUMANIA

Bartók, Béla (1881–1945)
*Mikrokosmos*. Books 1–6. Piano.
*Six Rumanian Folk Dances*. Piano; orchestral work.
*Two Rumanian Dances*. Opus 8a. Piano.

Enesco, Georges (1881–1955)
*Poème roumain*. Opus 1. Orchestral work.
*Rapsodies roumaines*. Opus 11. Orchestral work.

RUSSIA — see also Caucasian, Cities (Soviet)

Balakirev, Mily (1837–1910)
*Overture on Three Russian Themes.* Orchestral work.
Bartók, Béla (1881–1945)
"In Russian Style" from *Mikrokosmos.* Book 3. Piano.
Borodin, Alexander (1833–1887)
*In the Steppes of Central Asia.* Orchestral work.
*Prince Igor.* Opera.
Glazunov, Alexander (1865–1936)
*The Kremlin.* Opus 30. Orchestral work.
*Stenka Razin.* Opus 13. Orchestral work.
Glière, Reinhold (1875–1956)
"Russian Sailor's Dance" from *The Red Poppy.* Opus 70. Ballet.
Symphony No. 3 in B minor *Ilia Mourometz.* Opus 42.
Four movements: (1) "Wandering Pilgrims: Ilia Mourometz and
Sviatogar" (2) "Solovei the Brigand" (3) "The Palace of Prince
Vladimir" (4) "The Feats of Valor and the Petrification of Ilia
Mourometz."
Glinka, Mikhail (1804–1857)
*A Life for the Tsar.* Opera.
*Russlan and Ludmilla.* Opera.
*Ukranian Symphony.*
Haydn, Franz Joseph (1732–1809)
Quartets Nos. 37–42 *Russian.* Opus 33, Nos. 1–6. String quartets.
Ippolitov–Ivanov, Mikhail (1859–1965)
*On the Volga.* Opus 50. Small orchestra.
*The Year 1917.* Opus 71. Orchestral work.
Janácek, Leos (1854–1928)
*Taras Bulba.* Orchestral work.
Khachaturian, Aram (1903–1978)
*Gayane.* Suite No. 1. Ballet. Eight movements: (1) "Sabre Dance"
(2) "Dance of Ayshe" (3) "Dance of the Rose Maidens"
(4) "Dance of the Kurds" (5) "Lullaby" (6) "Dance of the Young
Kurds" (7) "Variations (8) "Lezghinska."
*Gayane.* Suite No. 2. Ballet. Four movements: (1) "Russian Dance"
(2) "Introduction" (3) "Gayane's Adagio" (4) "Fire."
*Russian Fantasy.* Orchestral work.
Liadov, Anatol (1855–1914)
*Eight Russian Folksongs.* Opus 58. Orchestral work.
Eight movements: (1) "Religious Chant" (2) "Christmas Carol"
(3) "Plaintive Melody" (4) "Humorous Song" (5) "Legend of the
Birds" (6) "Cradle Song" (7) "Round Dance" (8) "Village Dance
Song."
Loeffler, Charles Martin (1861–1935)
*Memories of my Childhood* (Life in a Russian Village). Orchestral
work.
Mussorgsky, Modest (1839–1881)
*Boris Godunov.* Opera.

*Impressions de voyage: En Crimée* (Travel impressions: Crimea). Piano.

*Pictures at an Exhibition.* Piano; orchestral work. Eleven movements: (1) "Promenade" (2) "Gnomes" (3) "The Old Castle" (4) "Tuileries" (5) "Bydlo" (6) "Ballet of the Chicks in their Shells" (7) "Samuel Goldenberg and Schmuyle" (8) "The Market Place at Limoges" (9) "Catacombs" (10) "A Hut on Fowl's Legs" (Baba Yaga) (11) "The Great Gate at Kiev." (Inspired by Victor Hartmann.)

Prokofiev, Sergei (1891–1953)
  *Alexander Nevsky.* Opus 78. Film music.
  *Le Pas d'acier* (The age of steel). Opus 41a. Ballet. Six movements: (1) "Train of Men Carrying Bags" (2) "Sailor with Bracelet and Working Women" (3) "Reconstruction of Scenery" (4) "The Factory" (5) "The Hammer" (6) "The Final Scene."
  *Russian Overture.* Opus 72. Orchestral work.

Rimsky–Korsakov, Nikolai (1844–1908)
  *Russian Easter Overture.* Opus 36. Orchestral work.
  *Sinfonietta on Russian Themes.* Opus 31. Orchestral work.
  *The Tsar's Bride.* Opera.

Rubinstein, Anton (1829–1894)
  *Ivan the Terrible.* Opus 79. Orchestral work.
  *Russia.* Orchestral work.

Saint–Saëns, Camille (1835–1921)
  *Caprice on Danish and Russian Airs.* Opus 79. Flute, oboe, clarinet and piano.

Shostakovich, Dmitri (1906–1975)
  *A Lady Macbeth of Mtsensk.* Opus 29. Opera.
  Symphony No. 2 *October.* Opus 14.
  Symphony No. 3 *First of May.* Opus 20.
  Symphony No. 5 (A Soviet artist's reply to just criticism). Opus 47.
  Symphony No. 11 (Year 1905). Opus 103. Four movements: (1) "Palace Square" (2) "January 9" (3) "Eternal Memory" (4) "Alarm."
  Symphony No. 12 *Lenin.* Opus 112.
  Symphony No. 13 *Babi Yar.* Opus 113.
  *The Age of Gold.* Opus 22. Ballet.

Stravinsky, Igor (1882–1971)
  *Song of the Haulers on the Volga.* Wind instruments.

Tchaikovsky, Peter Ilyich (1840–1893)
  *1812 Overture.* Opus 49. Orchestral work.
  "Russian Dance" from *The Nutcracker.* Opus 71. Ballet.
  Symphony No. 2 in C minor *Little Russian.* Opus 17.

Tcherepnin, Alexander (1899–1977)
  *Georgiana.* Opus 92. Piano and strings. Five movements: (1) "Ceremonial" (2) "Veils and Daggers" (3) "Chota and Thamor" (4) "Kartsuli" (5) "Apotheosis."

# S

## SAILING

Britten, Benjamin (1913–1976)
"Sailing" from *Holiday Diary*. Opus 5. Piano.
Debussy, Claude (1862–1918)
"Voiles" (Sails) from *Préludes I*. Piano.

## SAILORS — see also Ocean, Sailing, Ships

Auric, George
*Les Matelots* (The sailors). Ballet.
Bernstein, Leonard (1918–
*Fancy Free*. Ballet.
Britten, Benjamin (1913–1976)
*Billy Budd*. Opera.
Glière, Reinhold (1875–1956)
"Russian Sailors' Dance" from *The Red Poppy*. Opus 70. Ballet.
Prokofiev, Sergei (1891–1953)
"Sailor with Bracelet and Working Women" from *Le Pas d'acier* (The age of steel). Opus 41a. Ballet.
Rimsky–Korsakov, Nikolai (1844–1908)
"The Sea and Sinbad's Ship" from *Scheherazade*. Opus 35. Orchestral work.
Wagner, Richard (1813–1883)
*Der fliegende Holländer* (The flying Dutchman). Opera.
Walton, William (1902–1983)
*Portsmouth Point*. Orchestral work.

## SAINTS — see Religious Figures

## SCHOOL

Brahms, Johannes (1833–1897)
*Akademische Festouvertüre* (Academic Festival Overture). Opus 80. Orchestral work.

Haydn, Franz Joseph (1732–1809)
   Symphony No. 55 in E–flat major *Der Schulmeister*
   (The Schoolmaster).
   Symphony No. 92 in G major *Oxford*.


## SCOTLAND

Berlioz, Hector (1803–1869)
   *Waverley*. Opus 2. Orchestral work.
Brahms, Johannes (1833–1897)
   Ballade in D minor. Opus 10, No. 1. (Inspired by ballad *Edward*.)
   Piano.
Britten, Benjamin (1913–1976)
   *Scottish Ballad*. Opus 26. Two pianos and orchestra.
Bruch, Max (1838–1920)
   *Scottish Fantasy*. Opus 46. Violin and orchestra.
   *Scottish Fantasy*. Opus 64. Violin and harp.
Chadwick, George (1854–1931)
   *Tam O'Shanter*. Orchestral work.
MacCunn, Hamish (1868–1916)
   *The Land of the Mountain and the Flood*. Opus 8. Orchestral work.
Mackenzie, Alexander (1847–1935)
   Concerto in G major *Scottish*. Opus 55. Piano and orchestra.
   Scottish Rhapsody No. 1 *Rapsodie écossaise*. Opus 22. Orchestral
   work.
   Scottish Rhapsody No. 2 *Burns*. Opus 24. Orchestral work.
   Scottish Rhapsody No. 3 *Tam O'Shanter*. Opus 74. Orchestral work.
Mendelssohn, Felix (1809–1847)
   *The Hebrides* (Fingal's cave). Opus 26. Orchestral work.
   Symphony No. 3 in A minor *Scotch*. Opus 56.


SEA — see Ocean


SEASONS — see also Autumn, Spring, Summer, Winter

Glazunov, Alexander (1865–1936)
   *The Seasons*. Ballet.
Hadley, Henry (1871–1937)
   Symphony No. 2 *The Four Seasons*. Opus 30.
Malipiero, Gian Francesco (1882–1973)
   Symphony *The Four Seasons*. Four movements: (1) "Spring"
   (2) "Summer" (3) "Autumn" (4) "Winter."

Tchaikovsky, Peter Ilyich (1840–1893)
    *The Seasons*. Opus 37b. Piano. Twelve movements:
        (1) "January: By the Hearth" (2) "February: Carnival Time"
        (3) "March: Song of the Lark" (4) "April: Snowdrop"
        (5) "May: Bright Nights" (6) "June: Barcarolle"
        (7) "July: Reaper's Song" (8) "August: Harvest"
        (9) "September: The Hunt" (10) "October: Autumn
        Song" (11) "November: In the Troika" (12) "December:
        Christmas."
Vivaldi, Antonio (1678–1741)
    *Le quattro stagioni* (The four seasons). Opus 8. Violin and
    orchestra. Four movements: (1) "La Primavera" (Spring)
    (2) "L'Estate" (Summer) (3) "L'Autunno" (Autumn)
    (4) "L'Inverno" (Winter).


SHAKESPEARE — see also Shakespearean Characters

(Composers listed alphabetically after play)

*ALL'S WELL THAT ENDS WELL*

Hoérée, Arthur (1897–
    *All's Well that Ends Well*. Incidental music.

*ANTONY AND CLEOPATRA*

Barber, Samuel (1910–1981)
    *Antony and Cleopatra*. Opus 40. Opera.
Rubinstein, Anton (1829–1894)
    *Antony and Cleopatra*. Opus 116. Orchestral work.
Thomson, Virgil (1896–
    *Antony and Cleopatra*. Incidental music.

*AS YOU LIKE IT*

Bliss, Arthur (1891–1975)
    *As You Like It*. Incidental music.
Britten, Benjamin (1913–1976)
    *The Seven Ages of Man*. Incidental music.
Carpenter, John Alden (1876–1951)
    *The Seven Ages*. Orchestral work.
Henze, Hans Werner (1926–
    "Touchstone, Audrey and William" from *First Sonata on
        Shakespearean Characters*. Guitar.
Paine, John Knowles (1839–1906)
    *As You Like It*. Incidental music.

## A COMEDY OF ERRORS

Shaporin, Yuri (1887–1966)
*A Comedy of Errors.* Incidental music.

## CORIOLANUS

Mackenzie, Alexander (1847–1935)
*Coriolanus.* Opus 61. Incidental music.

## HAMLET

Blacher, Boris (1903–1975)
*Hamlet.* Opus 17. Orchestral work.
Bridge, Frank (1879–1941)
*There is a Willow Grows Aslant the Brook.* Small orchestra.
Gade, Niels (1817–1890)
*Hamlet.* Opus 37. Orchestral work.
Henze, Hans Werner (1926–
"Ophelia" from *First Sonata on Shakespearean Characters.* Guitar.
Joachim, Joseph (1831–1907)
*Hamlet.* Opus 4. Orchestral work.
Lekeu, Guillaume (1870–1894)
*Marche d'Ophélie.* Orchestral work.
Liszt, Franz (1811–1886)
*Hamlet.* Orchestral work.
MacDowell, Edward (1860–1908)
*Hamlet and Ophelia.* Opus 22. Orchestral work.
Shostakovich, Dmitri (1906–1975)
*Hamlet.* Opus 32. Incidental music.
Tchaikovsky, Peter Ilyich (1840–1893)
*Hamlet.* Opus 67. Orchestral work.

*HENRY IV* — see also Shakespearean Characters

Joachim, Joseph (1831–1907)
*Henry IV.* Opus 7. Orchestral work.

*HENRY V* — see also Shakespearean Characters

Walton, William (1902–1983)
*Henry V.* Film music.

## HENRY VIII

Sullivan, Arthur (1842–1900)
*Henry VIII.* Incidental music.

## JULIUS CAESAR

Castelnuovo–Tedesco, Mario (1895–1968)
*Julius Caesar.* Orchestral work.
Rózsa, Miklós (1907–
*Julius Caesar.* Incidental music.
Schumann, Robert (1810–1856)
*Julius Caesar.* Opus 128. Orchestral work.

## KING JOHN

Castelnuovo–Tedesco, Mario (1895–1968)
*King John.* Orchestral work.

## KING LEAR

Berlioz, Hector (1803–1869)
*Le Roi Lear.* Opus 4. Orchestral work.
Debussy, Claude (1862–1918)
*King Lear.* Incidental music.
Shaporin, Yuri (1887–1966)
*King Lear.* Incidental music.

## MACBETH

Bloch, Ernest (1880–1959)
*Macbeth.* Opera.
Henze, Hans Werner (1926–
"Mad Lady Macbeth" from *Second Sonata on Shakespearean Characters.* Guitar.
Khachaturian, Aram (1903–1978)
*Macbeth.* Incidental music.
Smetana, Bedrich (1824–1884)
*Macbeth and the Witches.* Piano.
Strauss, Richard (1864–1949)
*Macbeth.* Opus 23. Orchestral work.
Sullivan, Arthur (1842–1900)
*Macbeth.* Incidental music.
Verdi, Giuseppe (1813–1901)
*Macbeth.* Opera.

## MEASURE FOR MEASURE

Kabalevsky, Dmitri (1904–1987)
*Measure for Measure.* Incidental music.

## THE MERCHANT OF VENICE

Carter, Elliott (1908–
*The Merchant of Venice.* Incidental music.
Castelnuovo–Tedesco, Mario (1895–1968)
*The Merchant of Venice.* Orchestral work.
Humperdinck, Engelbert (1854–1921)
*The Merchant of Venice.* Incidental music.
Sullivan, Arthur (1842–1900)
*The Merchant of Venice.* Incidental music.

## THE MERRY WIVES OF WINDSOR

Nicolai, Otto (1810–1849)
*Die Lustigen Weiber von Windsor* (The Merry Wives of Windsor).
Opera.
Sullivan, Arthur (1842–1900)
*The Merry Wives of Windsor.* Incidental music.

## A MIDSUMMER NIGHT'S DREAM

Britten, Benjamin (1913–1976)
*A Midsummer Night's Dream.* Opera.
Castelnuovo–Tedesco, Mario (1895–1968)
*A Midsummer Night's Dream.* Orchestral work.
Henze, Hans Werner (1926–
"Bottom's Dream" from *Second Sonata on Shakespearean Characters.* Guitar.
"Oberon" from *First Sonata on Shakespearean Characters.* Guitar.
Mendelssohn, Felix (1809–1847)
*A Midsummer Night's Dream.* Opuses 21 and 61. Orchestral work.
Orff, Carl (1895–1982)
*A Midsummer Night's Dream.* Incidental music.

## MUCH ADO ABOUT NOTHING

Berlioz, Hector (1803–1869)
*Béatrice et Bénédict.* Opera.
Castelnuovo–Tedesco, Mario (1895–1968)
*Much Ado about Nothing.* Orchestral work.
Korngold, Erich (1897–1957)
*Much Ado about Nothing.* Opus 11. Incidental music.

*OTHELLO*

Coleridge–Taylor, Samuel (1875–1912)
*Othello.* Opus 79. Incidental music.
Dvorák, Antonín (1841–1904)
*Othello.* Opus 93. Orchestral work.
Hadley, Henry (1871–1937)
*Othello.* Opus 96. Orchestral work.
Rossini, Gioacchino (1792–1868)
*Otello.* Opera.
Verdi, Giuseppe (1813–1901)
*Otello.* Opera.

*RICHARD III*

Henze, Hans Werner (1926–
"Gloucester" from *First Sonata on Shakespearean Characters.*
Guitar.
Smetana, Bedrich (1824–1884)
*Richard III.* Opus 11. Orchestral work.
Walton, William (1902–1983)
*Richard III.* Film Music.

*ROMEO AND JULIET*

Berlioz, Hector (1803–1869)
*Roméo et Juliette.* Opus 17. Symphonic work with voice.
Blacher, Boris (1903–1975)
*Romeo und Julia.* Opera.
Diamond, David (1915–
*Romeo and Juliet.* Orchestral work. Five movements:
(1) "Overture" (2) "Balcony Scene" (3) "Romeo and Friar
Laurence" (4) "Juliet and her Nurse" (5) "Death of Romeo and
Juliet."
Gounod, Charles (1818–1893)
*Roméo et Juliette.* Opera.
Henze, Hans Werner (1926–
"Romeo and Juliet" from *First Sonata on Shakespearean
Characters.* Guitar.
Holbrooke, Joseph (1878–1958)
*Queen Mab.* Orchestral work.
Prokofiev, Sergei (1891–1953)
*Romeo and Juliet.* Opus 64–bis. Ballet. Seven movements:
(1) "Dance of the People" (2) "Scene" (3) "Madrigal"
(4) "Minuet" (5) "Masques" (6) "Romeo and Juliet"
(7) "The Death of Tybalt."

*Romeo and Juliet.* Opus 64–ter. Ballet. Seven movements:
(1) "Montagues and Capulets" (2) "Juliet, the Maiden"
(3) "Friar Laurence" (4) "Dance" (5) "The Parting of Romeo
and Juliet" (6) "Dance of the West Indian Slave Girls"
(7) "Romeo at Juliet's Grave."
*Romeo and Juliet.* Opus 101. Ballet. Six movements:
(1) "Romeo at the Fountain" (2) "The Morning Dance"
(3) "Juliet" (4) "The Nurse" (5) "Morning Serenade"
(6) "Juliet's Death."
Rorem, Ned (1923–
*Romeo and Juliet.* Flute and guitar.
Tchaikovsky, Peter Ilyich (1840–1893)
*Romeo and Juliet.* Orchestral work.

*THE TAMING OF THE SHREW*

Castelnuovo–Tedesco, Mario (1895–1968)
*The Taming of the Shrew.* Orchestral work.

*THE TEMPEST*

Foss, Lukas (1922–
*The Tempest.* Chamber orchestra.
Henze, Hans Werner (1926–
"Ariel" from *First Sonata on Shakespearean Characters.* Guitar.
Honegger, Arthur (1892–1955)
*The Tempest.* Orchestral work.
Locke, Matthew (1621–1677)
*The Tempest.* Incidental music.
Paine, John Knowles (1839–1906)
*The Tempest.* Orchestral work.
Sibelius, Jean (1865–1957)
*The Tempest.* Opus 109. Incidental music.
Sullivan, Arthur (1842–1900)
*The Tempest.* Opus 1. Incidental music.
Tchaikovsky, Peter Ilyich (1840–1893)
*The Tempest.* Opus 18. Orchestral work.

*TIMON OF ATHENS*

Diamond, David (1915–
*Timon of Athens.* Orchestral work.
Sullivan, Arthur (1842–1900)
*Timon of Athens.* Orchestral work.

*TWELFTH NIGHT*

Castelnuovo–Tedesco, Mario (1895–1968)
*Twelfth Night.* Orchestral work.
Henze, Hans Werner (1926–
"Sir Andrew Aguecheek" from *Second Sonata on Shakespearean
Characters.* Guitar.
Humperdinck, Engelbert (1854–1921)
*Twelfth Night.* Incidental music.

*THE WINTER'S TALE*

Castelnuovo–Tedesco, Mario (1895–1968)
*The Winter's Tale.* Orchestral work.
Humperdinck, Engelbert (1854–1921)
*The Winter's Tale.* Incidental music.
Suk, Josef (1874–1935)
*A Winter's Tale.* Opus 9. Orchestral work.


# SHAKESPEAREAN CHARACTERS — see also Shakespeare

Elgar, Edward (1857–1934)
*Falstaff.* Opus 68. Orchestral work. Four sections:
(1) "Falstaff and Prince Henry" (2) "Eastcheap – Gadshill – The
Boar's Head, Revelry and Sleep" (3) "Falstaff's March – The
Return through Gloucestershire – The New King – The Hurried
Ride to London" (4) "King Henry's Progress – The Repudiation
of Falstaff and his Death."
Henze, Hans Werner (1926–
*First Sonata on Shakespearean Characters.* Guitar. Six movements:
(1) "Gloucester" (2) "Romeo and Juliet" (3) "Ariel" (4) "Ophelia"
(5) "Touchstone, Audrey and William" (6) "Oberon."
*Second Sonata on Shakespearean Characters.* Guitar.
Three movements: (1) "Sir Andrew Aguecheek"
(2) "Bottom's Dream" (3) "Mad Lady Macbeth."
Verdi, Giuseppe (1813–1901)
*Falstaff.* Opera.


# SHEPHERD and SHEPHERDESS

Beethoven, Ludwig van (1770–1827)
"The Shepherd's Song" from Symphony No. 6 in F major *Pastorale.*
Opus 68.

Debussy, Claude (1862–1918)
  "The Little Shepherd" from *Children's Corner*. Piano.
Grieg, Edvard (1843–1907)
  "Shepherd's Boy" from *Lyric Suite*. Opus 54. Piano; orchestral work.

## SHIPS

Bartók, Béla (1881–1945)
  "Boating" from *Mikrokosmos*. Book 5. Piano.
Bloch, Ernest (1880–1959)
  "1620. The Soil – the Indians – the Mayflower – the Landing Pilgrims" from *America: An Epic Rhapsody*. Orchestral work.
Mendelssohn, Felix (1809–1847)
  "Venetianisches Gondellied" (Venetian gondola song) from *Lieder ohne Worte* (Songs without words). Opus 19, No. 6; Opus 30, No. 6; Opus 62, No. 5.
Ravel, Maurice (1875–1937)
  "Une Barque sur l'océan" (A boat on the ocean) from *Miroirs* (Mirrors). Piano.
Rimsky–Korsakov, Nikolai (1844–1908)
  "The Sea and Sinbad's Ship" from *Scheherazade*. Opus 35. Orchestral work.
Satie, Erik (1866–1925)
  "Yachting" from *Sports et divertissements* (Sports and entertainments). Piano.
Wagner, Richard (1813–1883)
  *Der fliegende Holländer* (The flying Dutchman). Opera.

## SIRENS — see also Greek Myths

Debussy, Claude (1862–1918)
  "Sirènes" from *Nocturnes*. Orchestral work.
Glière, Reinhold (1875–1956)
  *The Sirens*. Opus 33. Orchestral work.
Szymanowski, Karol (1882–1937)
  "The Island of Sirens" from *Metopes*. Opus 29. Piano.
Waldteufel, Emile (1837–1915)
  *Les Sirènes* (The sirens). Opus 154. Waltz.

SLAVIC — see also Hungary, Rumania

Bartók, Béla (1881–1945)
   "Evening in Transylvania" from *Ten Easy Pieces*. Piano.
   *Mikrokosmos*. Books 1–6. Piano.
Dvořák, Antonín (1841–1904)
   *Czech Suite*. Opus 39. Orchestral work.
   *Slavonic Dances*. Opus 46, 72. Orchestral work; piano duet.
Janácek, Leos (1854–1928)
   *Moravian Dances*. Orchestral work.
Tchaikovsky, Peter Ilyich (1840–1893)
   *Marche Slave*. Opus 31. Orchestral work.


SLEEP — see also Dream

Bellini, Vincenzo (1801–1835)
   *La Sonnambula* (The sleepwalker). Opera.
Elgar, Edward (1857–1934)
   "Elaine Asleep" from *King Arthur Suite*. Orchestral work.
   "Slumber Scene" from *Wand of Youth*. Opus 1a. Orchestral work.
Franck, César (1822–1890)
   "Psyche's Sleep" from *Psyché*. Orchestral work.
Liadov, Anatol (1855–1914)
   "Cradle Song" from *Eight Russian Folksongs*. Opus 58. Orchestral
      work.
Schumann, Robert (1810–1856)
   "Kind im Einschlummern" (Child falling asleep) from *Kinderscenen*
      (Scenes from childhood). Opus 15. Piano.
Tchaikovsky, Peter Ilyich (1840–1893)
   *La Belle au bois dormant* (Sleeping beauty). Opus 66. Ballet.


SNOW — see also Clouds, Rain, Storm, Water, Weather, Wind

Debussy, Claude (1862–1918)
   "Des Pas sur la neige" (Footsteps in the snow) from *Préludes I*. Piano.
   "Snow is Dancing" from *Children's Corner*. Piano.
Liszt, Franz (1811–1886)
   "Chasse–neige" (Snow plough) from *Etudes d'exécution transcendante*
      (Transcendental Etudes). Piano.
Rimsky–Korsakov, Nikolai (1844–1908)
   *The Snow Maiden*. Opera.
Tchaikovsky, Peter Ilyich (1840–1893)
   "April: Snowdrop" from *The Seasons*. Opus 37b. Piano.

SOLDIERS — see also Military, War, Weapons

Prokofiev, Sergei (1891–1953)
*Lieutenant Kije.* Opus 60. Orchestral work. Five movements:
(1) "The Birth of Kije" (2) "Romance" (3) "Kije's Wedding"
(4) "Troika" (5) "Burial of Kije."
Schumann, Robert (1810–1856)
"Soldatenmarsch" (Soldier's march) from *Album für die Jugend*
(Album for the young). Opus 68. Piano.
Stravinsky, Igor (1882–1971)
*L'Histoire du soldat* (A soldier's tale). Ballet. Nine movements:
(1) "Soldier's March" (2) "Soldier's Violin" (3) "Pastorale"
(4) "Royal March" (5) "Little Concerto" (6) "Three Dances"
(7) "Devil's Dance" (8) "Grand Chorale" (9) "Triumphal March
of the Devil."

SOUTH AMERICAN — see Brazil, Latin America

SOVIET UNION — see Russia

SPAIN — see also Cities (Spanish)

Albéniz, Isaac (1860–1909)
*Cantos de España* (Songs of Spain). Opus 232. Piano.
Five movements: (1) "Preludio" (2) "Oriental" (3) "Bajo la
palmera" (Under the palm tree) (4) "Córdoba" (5) "Seguidillas."
*Catalonia.* Piano.
*Iberia.* Book I. "Evocación," "El Puerto" (The port), "El Corpus
en Sevilla" (Festival in Seville). Piano.
*Iberia.* Book II. "Rondeña," "Almería," "Triana." Piano.
*Iberia.* Book III. "El Albaicín," "El Polo," "Lavapies." Piano.
*Iberia.* Book IV. "Málaga," "Jérez," "Eritaña." Piano.
*Navarra.* Piano.
*Rapsodie española* (Spanish rhapsody). Piano and orchestra.
*Suite española* (Spanish suite). Opus 47. Piano. Eight movements:
(1) "Granada" (2) "Cataluña" (3) "Sevilla" (4) "Cádiz"
(5) "Asturias" (6) "Aragón" (7) "Casilla" (8) "Cuba."
Carpenter, John Alden (1876–1951)
*The Birthday of the Infanta.* Ballet. Three movements:
(1) "The Guest" (2) "The Infanta" (3) "The Games."

Castelnuovo–Tedesco, Mario (1895–1968)
*The Birthday of the Infanta.* Ballet. Seven movements:
(1) "Fanfare" (2) "Sarabande of the King of Spain" (3) "Pavane of the Infanta" (4) "Ronde of Las Meninas" (5) "Minuet of the Rose" (6) "Dance of the Mirror" (7) "Epilogue."
Chabrier, Emmanuel (1841–1894)
*España* (Spain). Orchestral work.
Chaminade, Cecile (1857–1944)
*Sérénade espagnole* (Spanish serenade). Violin and piano.
Debussy, Claude (1862–1918)
*Iberia.* Orchestral work. Three movements: (1) "Par les rues et par les chemins" (In the streets and the byways) (2) "Les Parfums de la nuit" (Perfumes of the night) (3) "Le Matin d'un jour de fête" (The morning of a festival day).
Falla, Manuel de (1876–1946)
*Fantasía bética.* Piano.
*Noches en los jardines de España* (Nights in the gardens of Spain). Piano and orchestra. Three movements: (1) "En el Generalife" (At the Generalife) (2) "Danza lejana" (A far–off dance) (3) "En los jardines de la Sierra de Córdoba" (In the gardens of the Sierra of Cordoba).
*Pièces espagnoles* (Spanish pieces). Piano. Four movements: (1) "Aragonesa" (2) "Cubana" (3) "Montañesa" (4) "Andaluza."
Granados, Enrique (1867–1916)
*Danzas españoles* (Spanish dances). Books 1–4. Piano.
*Goyescas.* Piano. Six movements: (1) "Los requiebros" (Gallant compliments) (2) "Coloquio en la reja" (Conversation through the grilled window) (3) "El Fandango del candil" (Fandango by candlelight) (4) "Quejas o la maja y el ruiseñor" (The maid and the nightingale) (5) "El Amor y la muerte" (Love and death) (6) "Epílogo: la serenade del espectro" (Serenade of the specter). (Inspired by Goya.)
Lalo, Edouard (1823–1892)
*Symphonie espagnole* (Spanish symphony). Opus 21. Violin and orchestra.
Lecuona, Ernesto (1896–1963)
"Malagueña" from *Suite Andalucia.* Piano.
Massenet, Jules (1842–1912)
*Le Cid.* Opera.
Piston, Walter (1894–1976)
"Spanish Dance" from *The Incredible Flutist.* Ballet.
Ravel, Maurice (1875–1937)
*Rapsodie espagnole* (Spanish rhapsody). Orchestral work. Four movements: (1) "Prélude à la nuit" (Prelude of the night) (2) "Malagueña" (3) "Habanera" (4) "Feria" (fair).
Rimsky–Korsakov, Nikolai (1844–1908)
*Capriccio español* (Spanish caprice). Opus 34. Orchestral work.

Sarasate, Pablo de (1844–1908)
*Danses españoles* (Spanish dances). Opuses 21, 22, 23, 26. Violin and piano.
*Habanera*. Opus 21, No. 2. Violin and piano.
*Malagueña*. Opus 21, No. 1. Violin and piano.
Turina, Joaquín (1882–1949)
*Danzas fantásticas*. Opus 22. Orchestral work; piano.
Three movements: (1) "Exultación" (2) "Ensueño" (Musing) (3) "Orgía" (Orgy).
*L'Oración del torero* (The bullfighter's prayer). Opus 34. String quartet.
*La Procesión del Rocio* (The procession of the dew). Opus 9. Orchestral work.
*Mujeres españolas* (Spanish women). Opus 17. Piano.
Three movements: (1) "La Madrilena classica" (The classic woman of Madrid) (2) "La Anduluza sentimental" (The sentimental woman of Anduluza) (3) "La Corena coqueta" (The coquette of Corena).
"Sacro Monte" (Sacred mountain) from *Danzas gitanas*. Opus 55. Piano.
*Sanlúcar de Barrameda*. Opus 24. Piano. Four movements:
(1) "En la torre del Castillo" (In the tower of the Citadel)
(2) "Siluetas de la calzada" (Portrait of a woman in shoes)
(3) "La Playa" (The seacoast) (4) "Los Pescadores in Bajo de Guía" (The fisherman in Bajo de Guía).
*Sevilla*. Opus 2. Piano. Three movements: (1) "Sous les orangers" (Under the orange trees) (2) "Le Jeudi saint à minuit" (Holy Thursday at midnight) (3) "La Feria" (Holiday).

SPINNING WHEEL — see also Machines

Dvořák, Antonín (1841–1904)
"In the Spinning Room" from *From The Bohemian Forest*. Opus 68. Piano duet.
*The Golden Spinning-Wheel*. Orchestral work.
Fauré, Gabriel (1845–1924)
"The Spinner" from *Pelléas et Mélisande*. Opus 80. Orchestral work.
Mendelssohn, Felix (1809–1847)
"Spinnerlied" (Spinning song) from *Lieder ohne Worte* (Songs without words). Opus 67, No. 4. Piano.
Saint–Saëns, Camille (1835–1921)
*Le Rouet d'Omphale* (Omphale's spinning wheel). Opus 31. Orchestral work.
Sibelius, Jean (1865–1957)
"Mélisande of the Spinning Wheel" from *Pelléas et Mélisande*. Opus 46. Orchestral work.

SPIRITS — see also Angels, Fairy World

Beethoven, Ludwig van (1770–1827)
  Trio in D major *Geistertrio* (Ghost). Opus 70, No. 1. Piano, violin and cello.
Gluck, Christoph Willibald (1714–1787)
  "Dance of the Blessed Spirits" from *Orfeo ed Euridice*. Orchestral work.
Granados, Enrique (1867–1916)
  "Epílogo: la serenada del espectro" (Serenade of the specter) from *Goyescas*. Piano.
Liadov, Anatol (1855–1914)
  *Kikimora*. Opus 63. Orchestral work.


SPORTS — see also Games

Bennett, Robert Russell (1894–1981)
  *A Symphony in D for the Dodgers*. Four movements:
      (1) "Brooklyn Wins" (2) "Brooklyn Loses" (3) "Scherzo" (4) "The Giants come to Town."
Debussy, Claude (1862–1918)
  *Jeux* (Games). Ballet.
Honegger, Arthur (1892–1955)
  *Mouvement symphonique No. 2: Rugby*. Orchestral work.
Satie, Erik (1866–1925)
  *Sports et divertissements* (Sports and entertainments). Piano.
      Twenty movements: (1) "La Balancoire" (The swing) (2) "La Chasse" (The hunt) (3) "Comédie italienne" (Italian comedy) (4) "La Mariée" (The bride) (5) "Colin–Maillard" (Pin the tail on the donkey) (6) "La Pêche" (Fishing) (7) "Yachting" (8) "Bain de mer" (Sea bathing) (9) "Le Carnaval" (The carnival) (10) "Le Golf" (11) "La Pieuvre" (The octopus) (12) "Les Courses" (The races) (13) "Les Quatre coins" (The four corners) (14) "Pique Nique" (Picnic) (15) "Water Chute" (16) "Le Tango" (17) "Traineau" (Sleigh) (18) "Flirt" (19) "Feu d'artifice" (Fireworks) (20) "Le Tennis."
Waldteufel, Emile (1837–1915)
  "Les Pantineurs" (The skaters). Opus 183. Orchestral work.


SPRING — see also Autumn, Seasons, Summer, Winter

Bax, Arnold (1883–1953)
  *Spring Fire*. Orchestral work.

Beethoven, Ludwig van (1770–1827)
  Sonata in G major *Spring*. Opus 30, No. 3. Violin and piano.
Bloch, Ernest (1880–1959)
  *Hiver–Printemps* (Winter–Spring). Orchestral work.
Brahms, Johannes (1833–1897)
  Sextet in B–flat major *Spring*. Opus 18. String sextet.
Copland, Aaron (1900–
  *Appalachian Spring*. Ballet.
Debussy, Claude (1862–1918)
  "Rondes de printemps" (Songs of spring) from *Images*. Orchestral
    work.
Delius, Frederick (1862–1934)
  "On Hearing the First Cuckoo in Spring" from *Two Pieces for Small
    Orchestra*.
  "The March of Spring" from *North Country Sketches*. Orchestral
    work.
Glazunov, Alexander (1865–1936)
  *The Seasons*. Ballet.
Goldmark, Carl (1830–1915)
  *Im Frühling* (In springtime). Opus 36.
Grieg, Edvard (1843–1907)
  "The Last Spring" from *Two Elegiac Melodies*. Opus 34. String
    orchestra.
  "To Spring" from *Lyric Pieces*. Opus 43, No. 6. Piano.
Hadley, Henry (1871–1937)
  "Spring" from Symphony No. 2 *The Four Seasons*. Opus 30.
Harris, Roy (1898–1979)
  *Kentucky Spring*. Orchestral work.
Malipiero, Gian Francesco (1882–1973)
  "Spring" from Symphony *The Four Seasons*.
Mendelssohn, Felix (1809–1847)
  "Frühlingslied" (Spring song) from *Lieder ohne Worte* (Songs
    without words). Opus 62, No. 6. Piano.
Milhaud, Darius (1892–1974)
  *Le Printemps* (Spring). Violin and piano.
  Symphony No. 1 *Le Printemps* (Spring). Small orchestra.
Respighi, Ottorino (1879–1936)
  "Primavera" (Spring) from *Trittico botticelliano* (Botticellian
    triptych). Orchestral work.
Schumann, Robert (1810–1856)
  Symphony No. 1 in B–flat major *Spring*. Opus 38.
Sinding, Christian (1856–1941)
  *Rustle of Spring*. Opus 23, No. 3. Piano.

Stravinsky, Igor (1882–1971)
*Le Sacre du printemps* (The rite of spring). Ballet.
Part I: The Adoration of the Earth. Introduction – Harbingers of
Spring – Dance of the Adolescents – Spring Rounds – Games of
the Round Cities – The procession of the Wise Men – The
Adoration of the Earth – Dance of the Earth.
Part II: The Sacrifice. Introduction – Mysterious Circle of the
Adolescents – Glorification of the Chosen One – Evocation of
the Ancestors – The Sacrificial Dance of the Chosen One.
Vivaldi, Antonio (1678–1741)
"La Primavera" (Spring) from *Le quattro stagioni* (The four seasons).
Opus 8. Concerto for orchestra.
Zamfir, Gheorghe (1941–
*Rhapsodie du printemps* (Rhapsody for spring). Panpipes and
orchestra.


STARS — see Universe


STORM — see also Rain, Snow, Weather, Wind

Beethoven, Ludwig van (1770–1827)
"The Storm" from Symphony No. 6 in F major *Pastoral*.
Opus 68.
Britten, Benjamin (1913–1976)
"The Storm" from *Four Sea Interludes* from *Peter Grimes*. Orchestral
work.
Copland, Aaron (1900–
*The Second Hurricane*. Opera.
Grofé, Ferde (1892–1972)
"Cloudburst" from *Grand Canyon Suite*. Orchestral work.
Haydn, Franz Joseph (1732–1809)
Symphony No. 8 in G major *La Tempesta* (The storm).
Liszt, Franz (1811–1886)
"Orage" (Storm) from *Années de pèlerinage: Première année: Suisse*
(Years of pilgrimage: first year: Switzerland). Piano.
Rieti, Vittorio (1898–
"The Flood" from *L'Arca di Noé* (Noah's Ark). Orchestral work.
Strauss, Johann Jr. (1825–1899)
*Unter Donner und Blitz* (Thunder and lightning). Opus 324. Waltz.

# STREETS

Copland, Aaron (1900–)
"Street in Frontier Town" from *Billy the Kid*. Ballet.
Debussy, Claude (1862–1918)
"Par les rues et par les chemins" (In the streets and by the waysides)
from *Iberia*. Orchestral work.
Elgar, Edward (1857–1934)
*Cockaigne* (In London town). Opus 40. Orchestral work.
Revueltas, Silvestre (1899–1940)
*Caminos* (Roads). Orchestral work.

# SUMMER — see also Autumn, Seasons, Spring, Winter

Alfvén, Hugo (1872–1960)
*Midsommarvaka* (Midsummer vigil). Orchestral work.
Barber, Samuel (1910–1981)
*Summer Music*. Opus 31. Woodwinds.
Bridge, Frank (1879–1941)
*Summer*. Orchestral work.
Debussy, Claude (1862–1918)
"Pour invoquer Pan, Dieu du vent d'été" (To invoke Pan, God of the
summer wind) from *Six Epigraphes antiques* (Six ancient
inscriptions). Piano duet.
Delius, Frederick (1862–1934)
*A Song of Summer*. Orchestral work.
*In a Summer Garden*. Orchestral work.
"Summer Night on the River" from *Two Pieces for Small Orchestra*.
Glazunov, Alexander (1865–1936)
*The Seasons*. Ballet.
Glinka, Mikhail (1804–1857)
*Summer Night in Madrid*. Orchestral work.
Hadley, Henry (1871–1937)
"Summer" from Symphony No. 2 *The Four Seasons*. Opus 30.
Honegger, Arthur (1892–1955)
*Pastorale d'été* (Summer pastoral). Orchestral work.
Indy, Vincent d' (1851–1931)
*Jour d'été à la montagne* (Summer day on the mountain). Opus 61.
Piano and orchestra. Three movements: (1) "L'Aube" (Dawn)
(2) "Le Jour" (Day) (3) "Le Soir" (Evening).
Kodály, Zoltán (1882–1967)
*Nyári este* (Summer evening). Orchestral work.
Malipiero, Gian Francesco (1882–1973)
"Summer" from Symphony *The Four Seasons*.
Mendelssohn, Felix (1809–1847)
*A Midsummer Night's Dream*. Opus 21 and 61a. Orchestral work.

Piston, Walter (1894–1976)
"Summer Evening" from *Three New England Sketches*. Orchestral
work.
Prokofiev, Sergei (1891–1953)
*Summer Day*. Opus 65b. Orchestral work. Seven Movements:
(1) "Morning" (2) "Tag" (3) "Waltz" (4) "Regrets" (5) "March"
(6) "Evening" (7) "Moonlit Meadows."
Vivaldi, Antonio (1678–1741)
"L'Estate" (Summer) from *Le quattro stagioni* (The four seasons).
Opus 8. Violin and orchestra.

## SUN — see also Sunrise, Sunset

Elgar, Edward (1857–1934)
"Sun Dance" from *Wand of Youth Suite* No. 1a. Orchestral work.
Haydn, Franz Joseph (1732–1809)
Quartets Nos. 1–6 *Sonnenquartette* (Sun Quartets). Opus 20. String
quartets.

## SUNRISE — see also Sunset

Britten, Benjamin (1913–1976)
"Dawn" from *Four Sea Interludes* from *Peter Grimes*. Orchestral
work.
Debussy, Claude (1862–1918)
"De l'aube à midi sur la mer" (From dawn to noon on the sea) from
*La Mer* (The sea). Orchestral work.
Grofé, Ferde (1892–1972)
"Sunrise" from *Grand Canyon Suite*. Orchestral work.
Hanson, Howard (1896–1981)
*Before the Dawn*. Opus 17. Orchestral work.
Haydn, Franz Joseph (1732–1809)
Quartet No. 78 in B–flat major *Sunrise*. Opus 76, No. 4. String
quartet.
Indy, Vincent d' (1851–1931)
"L'Aube" (Dawn) from *Jour d'été à la montagne* (Summer day on the
mountain). Opus 61. Piano and orchestra.
Respighi, Ottorino (1879–1936)
"La Fontana di Valle Giulia all' alba" (The fountain of Valle Giulia at
dawn) from *Fontane di Roma* (Fountains of Rome). Orchestral
work.
Sibelius, Jean (1865–1957)
*Night Ride and Sunrise*. Opus 55. Orchestral work.

SUNSET — see also Sunrise

Grofé, Ferde (1892–1972)
"Sunset" from *Grand Canyon Suite*. Orchestral work.
Respighi, Ottorino (1879–1936)
"La Fontana di Villa Medici al tramonto" (The fountain of the Villa Medici at dusk) from *Fontane di Roma* (Fountains of Rome). Orchestral work.

SWEDEN

Alfvén, Hugo (1872–1960)
Swedish Rhapsody No. 1 *Midsommarvaka* (Midsummer vigil). Orchestral work.
Swedish Rhapsody No. 3 *Dalarhapsodien*. Opus 48. Orchestral work.
Atterberg, Kurt (1887–1974)
*Swedish Rhapsody*. Orchestral work.
*Varmland Rhapsody*. Opus 36. Orchestral work.
Hanson, Howard (1896–1981)
*Scandinavian Suite*. Opus 13. Piano. Three movements: (1) "Vermeland" (2) "Elegy" (3) "Clog Dance."
Symphony No. 1 *Nordic*. Opus 21.

SWITZERLAND

Indy, Vincent d' (1851–1931)
*Helvétia*. Opus 17. Piano. Three movements: (1) "Aarau" (2) "Schinznach" (3) "Laufenburg."
Liszt, Franz (1811–1886)
*Années de pèlerinage: Première année: Suisse* (Years of pilgrimage: first year: Switzerland). Piano. Nine movements: (1) "Chapelle de Guillaume Tell" (Chapel of William Tell) (2) "Au lac de Wallenstadt" (By the lake of Wallenstadt) (3) "Pastorale" (4) "Au bord d'une source" (On the edge of a spring) (5) "Orage" (Storm) (6) "Vallée d'Obermann" (Valley of Obermann) (7) "Eglogue" (Pastoral poem) (8) "Le Mal du pays" (Nostalgia) (9) "Les Cloches de Genève" (The bells of Geneva).
MacDowell, Edward (1860–1908)
"In Tyrol" from *Moon Pictures*. Opus 21. Piano duet.

# T

TALES — see also Fairy Tales, Folk Tales, Greek Myths, Literature

Chadwick, George (1854–1931)
*Rip Van Winkle*. Orchestral work. (Inspired by Washington Irving.)
Cowell, Henry (1897–1965)
*Tales of our Countryside*. Piano and orchestra. Four movements: (1) "Deep Tides" (2) "Exultation" (3) "The Harp of Life" (4) "Country Reel."
MacDowell, Edward (1860–1908)
*Fireside Tales*. Opus 61. Piano. Six movements: (1) "An Old Love Story" (2) "Of Brer Rabbit" (3) "From a German Forest" (4) "Of Salamanders" (5) "A Haunted House" (6) "By Smouldering Embers."
"From Uncle Remus" from *Woodland Sketches*. Opus 51. Piano.
Offenbach, Jacques (1819–1880)
*Les Contes d'Hoffman* (The tales of Hoffman). Opera.
Rimsky–Korsakov, Nikolai (1844–1908)
*Scheherazade*. Opus 35. Orchestral work. Four movements: (1) "The Sea and Sinbad's Ship" (2) "The Kalendar Prince" (3) "The Young Prince and the Princess" (4) "The Festival at Baghdad – The Sea – The Ship Founders on the Rock."
Strauss, Johann Jr. (1825–1899)
*Geschichten aus dem Wienerwald* (Tales from the Vienna Woods). Opus 325. Waltz.
Stravinsky, Igor (1882–1971)
*L'Histoire du soldat* (A soldier's tale). Ballet. Nine movements: (1) "Soldier's March" (2) "Soldier's Violin" (3) "Pastorale" (4) "Royal March" (5) "Little Concerto" (6) "Three Dances" (7) "Devil's Dance" (8) "Grand Chorale" (9) "Triumphal March of the Devil."

# THEATRE

Bennett, Robert Russell (1894–1981)
*Overture to an Imaginary Drama*. Orchestral work.
Chadwick, George (1854–1931)
*Melpomene* (Muse of tragedy). Orchestral work.
*Thalia* (Muse of comedy). Orchestral work.
Copland, Aaron (1900–
*Music for the Theatre*. Orchestral work.

TIME — see also Clock

Cage, John (1912–
  4' 33".
Chopin, Frederic (1810–1849)
  Waltz in D–flat major *Minute.* Opus 64, No. 1. Piano.
Messiaen, Olivier (1908–
  *Quatuor pour la fin du temps* (Quartet for the end of time). Violin,
  clarinet, cello, piano. Eight movements: (1) "Liturgie de cristal"
  (Liturgy of crystal) (2) "Vocalise, pour l'ange qui annonce la fin du
  temps" (Vocalise, for the angel who announces the end of time)
  (3) "Abîme des oiseaux" (Abyss of the birds) (4) "Intermède"
  (Interlude) (5) "Louange à l'éternité de Jésus" (Praise to the eternity
  of Jesus) (6) "Danse de la fureur, pour les sept trompettes" (Dance
  of fury, for the seven trumpets) (7) "Fouillis d'arcs–en–ciel, pour
  l'ange qui annonce la fin du temps" (Cluster of rainbows, for the
  angel who announces the end of time) (8) "Louange à l'immortalité
  de Jésus" (Praise to the immortality of Jesus).
Piston, Walter (1894–1976)
  "Eight O'Clock Strikes" from *The Incredible Flutist.* Ballet.
Ponchielli, Amilcare (1834–1886)
  "Dance of the Hours" from *La Gioconda.* Orchestral work.
Turina, Joaquín (1882–1949)
  "Le Jeudi Saint à minuit" (Holy Thursday at midnight) from *Sevilla.*
  Piano.


TOMB — see also Death

Dello Joio, Norman (1913–
  "The Tomb" from *New York Profiles.* Orchestral work.
Hindemith, Paul (1895–1963)
  "The Entombment" from *Mathis der Maler* (Matthias the painter).
  Opera; orchestral work.
Mussorgsky, Modest (1839–1881)
  "Catacombs" from *Pictures at an Exhibition.* Piano; orchestral work.


TRAGIC — see also Affections

Brahms, Johannes (1833–1897)
  *Tragische Ouvertüre* (Tragic overture). Opus 81. Orchestral work.
Chadwick, George (1854–1931)
  *Melpomene* (Muse of Tragedy). Orchestral work.
Mahler, Gustav (1860–1911)
  Symphony No. 6 in A minor *Tragic.*

Schubert, Franz (1797–1828)
Symphony in C minor *Tragic*.


TRAVELS — see also Vehicles

Bartók, Béla (1881–1945)
"Wandering" from *Mikrokosmos*. Book 3. Piano.
Grieg, Edvard (1843–1907)
"Ensom vandrer" (Lonely wanderer) from *Lyric Pieces*. Opus 43.
Piano.
Ibert, Jacques (1890–1962)
*Escales* (Ports). Orchestral work. Three movements:
(1) "Rome–Palerme" (2) "Tunis–Nefia" (3) "Valencia."
Liszt, Franz (1811–1886)
*Années de pèlerinage: Première année: Suisse* (Years of pilgrimage:
first year: Switzerland). Piano. Nine movements: (1) "Chapelle de
Guillaume Tell" (Chapel of William Tell) (2) "Au lac de Wallenstadt"
(By the lake of Wallenstadt) (3) "Pastorale" (4) "Au bord d'une
source" (On the edge of a spring) (5) "Orage" (Storm)
(6) "Vallée d'Obermann" (Valley of Obermann) (7) "Eglogue"
(Pastoral poem) (8) "Le Mal du pays" (Nostalgia)
(9) "Les Cloches de Genève" (The bells of Geneva).
*Années de pèlerinage: Seconde année: Italie* (Years of pilgrimage:
second year: Italy). Piano. Seven movements: (1) "Sposalizio"
(Wedding) (2) "Il Penseroso" (The thoughtful one)
(3) "Canzonetta del Salvator Rosa" (Song of Salvator Rosa)
(4) "Sonetto 47 del Petrarca" (Petrarch sonnet 47) (5) "Sonetto 104
del Petrarca" (Petrarch sonnet 104) (6) "Sonetto 123 del Petrarca"
(Petrarch sonnet 123) (7) "Après une lecture de Dante" (After
reading Dante).
*Années de pèlerinage: Troisième année* (Years of pilgrimage: third
year). Piano. Seven movements: (1) "Angelus"
(2) and (3) "Cyprès de la Villa d'Este" (Cypresses at the Villa
d'Este) (4) "Les Jeux d'eau à la Villa d'Este" (Fountains at the
Villa d'Este) (5) "Sunt lacrymae rerum" (6) "Marche funèbre"
(Funeral march) (7) "Sursum corda" (Lift up your hearts).
Mendelssohn, Felix (1809–1847)
*Meeresstille und glückliche Fahrt* (Calm sea and prosperous voyage).
Opus 27. Orchestral work.
Mussorgsky, Modest (1839–1881)
*Impressions de voyage: En Crimée* (Travel impressions: Crimea).
Piano.
Schubert, Franz (1797–1828)
Fantasy in C major *The Wanderer*. Opus 15. Piano.
Wagner, Richard (1813–1883)
"Siegfried's Rhine Journey" from *Götterdämmerung* (Twilight of the
Gods). Orchestral work.

# TREES — see also Forest, Leaves, Nature

Bax, Arnold (1883–1953)
*The Tale the Pine Trees Knew.* Orchestral work.
Castelnuovo–Tedesco, Mario (1895–1968)
*Cipressi* (Cypress). Orchestral work.
Gottschalk, Louis Moreau (1829–1869)
*Le Bananier* (The banana tree). Opus 5. Piano.
Liszt, Franz (1811–1886)
"Cyprès de la Villa d'Este" (Cypresses at the Villa d'Este) from
*Années de pèlerinage: Troisième année* (Years of pilgrimage: third
year). Piano.
MacDowell, Edward (1860–1908)
"To an Old White Pine" from *New England Idyls.* Opus 62. Piano.
Respighi, Ottorino (1879–1936)
*Pini di Roma* (Pines of Rome). Orchestral work. Four movements:
(1) "I Pini di Villa Borghese" (The pines of the Villa Borghese)
(2) "Pini presso una catacombe" (The pines near a catacomb)
(3) "I Pini del Gianicolo" (The pines of the Janiculum)
(4) "I Pini di Via Appia" (The pines of the Appian Way).
Revueltas, Silvestre (1899–1940)
*Colorines* (Mexican tree). Orchestral work.
Sibelius, Jean (1865–1957)
*Five Pieces.* Opus 75. Piano. Five movements: (1) "The Solitary Fir
Tree" (2) "When the Rowan–tree blooms" (3) "The Aspen"
(4) "The Birch Tree" (5) "The Spruce–Pine."
Turina, Joaquín (1882–1949)
"Sous les orangers" (Under the orange trees) from *Sevilla.* Opus 2.
Piano.

# TROJANS and TROY — see also Greek Myths

Berlioz, Hector (1803–1869)
*Les Troyens* (The trojans). Opera.
Purcell, Henry (1659–1695)
*Dido and Aeneas.* Opera.
Rameau, Jean–Philippe (1683–1764)
*Dardanus.* Opera.
Walton, William (1902–1983)
*Troilus and Cressida.* Opera.
Wolf, Hugo (1860–1903)
*Penthesilea.* Orchestral work. Three movements:
(1) "The Departure of Amazons for Troy" (2) "Penthesilea's Dream
of the Feast of the Roses" (3) "Combats, Passions, Frenzy,
Annihilation."

TROLLS — see Dwarfs

## TURKEY

Beethoven, Ludwig van (1770–1827)
"Marcia alla turca" (Turkish march) from *Die Ruinen von Athen* (The ruins of Athens). Opus 113. Orchestral work.
Boieldieu, François Adrien (1775–1834)
*The Caliph of Baghdad.* Opera.
Ippolitov–Ivanov, Mikhail (1859–1965)
*In the Steppes of Turkmenia.* Opus 65. Orchestral work.
*Turkish Fragments.* Opus 62. Orchestral work.
*Turkish March.* Opus 55. Orchestral work.
Mozart, Wolfgang Amadeus (1756–1791)
*Die Entführung aus dem Serail* (The abduction from the Seraglio). K. 384. Opera.
"Rondo alla turca" (Turkish march) from *Sonata in A major.* K. 331. Piano.

# U

UNITED STATES — see also Cities (New York), Cowboys

Bennett, Robert Russell (1894–1981)
*Suite of Old American Dances.* Wind ensemble.
Bloch, Ernest (1880–1959)
*America: An Epic Rhapsody.* Orchestral work. Three movements: (1) "1620. The Soil – the Indians – the Mayflower – the Landing Pilgrims" (2) "1861 – 1865. Hours of Joy – Hours of Sorrow" (3) "1926. The Present – the Future."
Carpenter, John Alden (1876–1951)
*Skyscrapers: A Ballet of American Life.* Ballet.
Castelnuovo–Tedesco, Mario (1895–1968)
*Nocturne in Hollywood.* Piano.
Converse, Frederick (1871–1940)
*California.* Orchestral work.
Copland, Aaron (1900–
*An Outdoor Overture.* Orchestral work.
*Appalachian Spring.* Ballet.
*Fanfare for the Common Man.* Orchestral work.

Cowell, Henry (1897–1965)
*Tales of our Countryside.* Piano and orchestra. Four movements:
(1) "Deep Tides" (2) "Exultation" (3) "The Harp of Life"
(4) "Country Reel."
Creston, Paul (1906–1985)
*Frontiers.* Opus 34. Orchestral work.
Delius, Frederick (1862–1934)
*Appalachia.* Orchestral work.
*Florida.* Orchestral work.
Dello Joio, Norman (1913–
*American Landscape.* Orchestral work.
Dvořák, Antonín (1841–1904)
Quartet in F major *American.* Opus 96. String quartet.
Symphony No. 9 in E minor *From the New World.* Opus 95.
Gilbert, Henry F. (1868–1928)
*Americanesque.* Orchestral work.
Gould, Morton (1913–
*American Salute.* Orchestral work.
Grofé, Ferde (1892–1972)
*Grand Canyon Suite.* Orchestral work. Five movements:
(1) "Sunrise" (2) "The Painted Desert" (3) "On the Trail"
(4) "Sunset" (5) "Cloudburst."
*Mississippi Suite.* Orchestral work. Four movements:
(1) "Father of Waters" (2) "Huckleberry Finn" (3) "Old Creole
Days" (4) "Mardi Gras."
Hanson, Howard (1896–1981)
*Merry Mount.* Opus 31. Opera; orchestral work.
Harris, Roy (1898–1979)
*American Creed.* Orchestral work.
*Kentucky Spring.* Orchestral work.
*Ten American Ballads.* Piano.
Ives, Charles (1874–1954)
*Holidays Symphony.* Four movements: (1) "Washington's
Birthday" (2) "Decoration Day" (3) "Fourth of July"
(4) "Thanksgiving or Forefathers' Day."
Sonata No. 2 *Concord.* Piano. Four movements: (1) "Emerson"
(2) "Hawthorne" (3) "The Alcotts" (4) "Thoreau."
Symphony No. 3 *The Camp Meeting.*
*Three Places in New England.* Orchestral work. Three movements:
(1) "Boston Common" (2) "Putnam's Camp" (3) "The Houstatonic
at Stockbridge."
MacDowell, Edward (1860–1908)
*New England Idyls.* Opus 62. Piano. Ten movements: (1) "An Old
Garden" (2) "Midsummer" (3) "Midwinter" (4) "With Sweet
Lavender" (5) "In Deep Woods" (6) "Indian Idyl" (7) "To an Old
White Pine" (8) "From Puritan Days" (9) "From a Log Cabin"
(10) "The Joy of Autumn."
McDonald, Harl (1899–1955)
Symphony No. 1 *The Santa Fé Trail.*

Piston, Walter (1894–1976)
*Three New England Sketches*. Orchestral work. (1) "Seaside"
(2) "Summer Evening" (3) "Mountains."
Read, Gardner (1913–
*Pennsylvania*. Opus 67. Orchestral work.
Schuman, William (1910–
*American Festival Overture*. Orchestral work.
*New England Triptych*. (Three pieces for orchestra after William
Billings.) (1) "Be Glad then, America" (2) "When Jesus Wept"
(3) "Chester."
Siegmeister, Elie (1909–
*American Sonata*. Piano.
*Ozark Set*. Orchestral work. Four movements:
(1) "Morning in the Hills" (2) "Camp Meeting"
(3) "Lazy Afternoon" (4) "Saturday Night."
*Prairie Legend*. Orchestral work.
Thomson, Virgil (1896–
*Louisiana Story*. Orchestral work.


UNIVERSE — see also Earth, Moon, Sun

Hindemith, Paul (1895–1963)
*Die Harmonie der Welt* (The harmony of the world). Opera; orchestral
work. Three movements: (1) "Musica Instrumentalis"
(2) "Musica Humana" (3) "Musica Mundana." (Inspired by
Johannes Kepler.)
Holst, Gustav (1874–1934)
*The Planets*. Opus 32. Orchestral work. Seven movements:
(1) "Mars, the Bringer of War" (2) "Venus, the Bringer of
Peace" (3) "Mercury, the Winged Messenger" (4) "Jupiter, the
Bringer of Jollity" (5) "Saturn, the Bringer of Old Age"
(6) "Uranus, the Magician" (7) "Neptune, the Mystic."
Klami, Uuno (1900–1961)
*Aurora Borealis*. Opus 38. Orchestral work.
Messiaen, Olivier (1908–
"Amen of the Stars, of the Planet Saturn" from *Visions de l'amen*.
Two pianos.
Milhaud, Darius (1892–1974)
*La Création du monde* (The creation of the world). Ballet.

# V

VEHICLES — see also Ships, Transportation

Anderson, Leroy (1908–1975)
*Sleigh Ride.* Orchestral work.
Carpenter, John Alden (1876–1951)
*Adventures in a Perambulator.* Orchestral work. Six movements:
(1) "En Voiture" (Take your seat) (2) "The Policeman"
(3) "The Hurdy Gurdy" (4) "The Lake" (5) "The Dogs"
(6) "Dreams."
Copland, Aaron (1900–
"Subway Jam" from *Music for a Great City.* Orchestral work.
Honegger, Arthur (1892–1955)
*Mouvement symphonique No. 1: Pacific 231.* Orchestral work.
Ibert, Jacques (1890–1962)
"The Métro" from *Paris.* Orchestral work.
Milhaud, Darius (1892–1974)
*Le Train bleu* (The blue train). Ballet.
Mussorgsky, Modest (1839–1881)
"Bydlo" (Polish oxcart) from *Pictures at an Exhibition.* Piano;
orchestral work.
Satie, Erik (1866–1925)
"Traineau" (Sleigh) from *Sports et divertissements* (Sports and
entertainments). Piano.
Tchaikovsky, Peter Ilyich (1840–1893)
"November: In the Troika" from *The Seasons.* Opus 37b. Piano.
Villa–Lobos, Heitor (1887–1959)
"The Little Train to Caipira" from *Bachianas brasileiras.* No. 2.
Orchestral work.


VILLAGES and TOWNS — see also Cities

Bartók, Béla (1881–1945)
"Village Joke" from *Mikrokosmos.* Book 5. Piano.
"Village Song" from *Mikrokosmos.* Book 1. Piano.
Beethoven, Ludwig van (1770–1827)
"Village Festival" from Symphony No. 6 in F major *Pastoral.*
Opus 68.
Copland, Aaron (1900–
"Street in Frontier Town" from *Billy the Kid.* Ballet.
Ippolitov–Ivanov, Mikhail (1859–1965)
"In the Village" from *Caucasian Sketches.* Opus 10. Orchestral work.

Liadov, Anatol (1855–1914)
"Village Dance Song" from *Eight Russian Folk Songs.* Opus 58. Orchestral work.
MacDowell, Edward (1860–1908)
"Village Festival" from Suite No. 2 *Indian.* Opus 48. Orchestral work.

# W

WAR — see also Military, Soldiers, Weapons

Beethoven, Ludwig van (1770–1827)
*Wellingtons Sieg* (Wellington's victory) or *Battle Symphony.* Opus 91. Orchestral work. Two movements: (1) "The Battle" (2) "Victory Symphony."
Busoni, Ferruccio (1866–1924)
*Zweite Orchester–Suite Geharnischte Suite* [Second orchestral suite (Armor suite)]. Opus 34a. Orchestral work. Four movements: (1) "Vorspiel" (Prelude) (2) "Kriegstanz" (War dance) (3) "Grabdenkmal" (Tombstone) (4) "Ansturm" (Assault).
Byrd, William (1543–1623)
"The Battle" from *My Ladye Nevells Booke.* Harpsichord. Nine movements: (1) "The Soldier's Summons" (2) "The March of Footmen" (3) "The March of Horsemen" (4) "The Trumpets" (5) "The Irish March" (6) "The Bagpipe and the Drone" (7) "The Flute and the Drum" (8) "The March to the Fight" (9) "The Retreat."
Chopin, Frederic (1810–1849)
*Ballade No. 1 in G minor.* Opus 23. Piano. (Inspired by Konrad Valenrod.)
Copland, Aaron (1900–
"Gun Battle" from *Billy the Kid.* Ballet.
Creston, Paul (1906–1985)
*Chant of 1942.* Orchestral work.
Elgar, Edward (1857–1934)
"Battle Scene" from *King Arthur Suite.* Orchestral work.
Harris, Roy (1898–1979)
"Civil War, Brother against Brother" from Symphony No. 10 *Abraham Lincoln.*
Holst, Gustav (1874–1934)
"Mars, the Bringer of War" from *The Planets.* Opus 32. Orchestral work.
Kodály, Zoltán (1882–1967)
"The Battle and Defeat of Napoleon" from *Háry János.* Orchestral work.

Liszt, Franz (1811–1886)
*Hunnenschlacht* (The Battle of the Huns). Orchestral work.
MacDowell, Edward (1860–1908)
"In War–time" from Suite No. 2 *Indian*. Opus 48. Orchestral work.
Malipiero, Gian Francesco (1882–1973)
*Pause del silenzio* (Silent pause). Orchestral work.
Seven movements: (1) "Melancholy Pastorale" (2) "Fantastic
Scene" (3) "Strange Serenade" (4) "A Sinister Ride"
(5) "Funeral March" (6) "Mysterious Calls"
(7) "Lugubrious Orgy."
Prokofiev, Sergei (1891–1953)
Sonata No. 6 in A major *War*. Opus 82. Piano.
Sonata No. 7 in B–flat major *Stalingrad*. Opus 83. Piano.
Sonata No. 8 in B–flat major *War*. Opus 84. Piano.
*War and Peace*. Opus 91. Opera.
Schelling, Ernest (1876–1939)
*A Victory Ball*. Orchestral work.
Schuman, William (1910–
*Prayer in Time of War*. Orchestral work.
Schumann, Robert (1810–1856)
"Kriegslied" (War song) from *Album für die Jugend* (Album for
the young). Opus 68. Piano.
Shostakovich, Dmitri (1906–1975)
Quartet No. 8 in C minor (In Memory of Victims of Fascism
and War). Opus 110. String quartet.
Strauss, Richard (1864–1949)
"The Hero's Battlefield" from *Ein Heldenleben* (A hero's life). Opus
40. Orchestral work.
Tchaikovsky, Peter Ilyich (1840–1893)
*1812 Overture*. Opus 49. Orchestral work.
Wolf, Hugo (1860–1903)
"Combats, Passions, Frenzy, Annihilation" from *Penthesilea*.
Orchestral work.


WATER — see also Fountains, Lakes, Nature, Ocean, Rain, Rivers,
Snow, Storm, Waves

Cherubini, Luigi (1760–1842)
*Les Deux journées* (The water carrier). Opera.
Debussy, Claude (1862–1918)
"Reflets dans l'eau" (Reflections on the water) from *Images I*.
Piano.
Handel, George Frideric (1685–1759)
*Water Music*. Orchestral work.

Liszt, Franz (1811–1886)
"Au bord d'une source" (On the edge of a spring) from *Années de pèlerinage: Première année: Suisse* (Years of pilgrimage: first year: Switzerland). Piano.
Rorem, Ned (1923–
*Water Music*. Orchestral work.


WAVES — see also Water

Bartók, Béla (1881–1945)
"Waves" from *Mikrokosmos*. Book 2. Piano.
Liszt, Franz (1811–1886)
"St. François de Paule marchant sur les flots" (St. Francis of Paola walking on the waves) from *Légendes*. Piano.
Reger, Max (1873–1916)
"Im Spiel der Wellen" (Among the play of the waves) from *Vier Tondichtungen nach Arnold Böcklin* (Four tone poems after Arnold Böcklin). Opus 128. Orchestral work.


WEAPONS — see also Military, Soldiers, War

Esplá, Oscar (1886–1976)
*Don Quixote velando las armas* (Don Quixote watching over his arms). Orchestral work.
Khachaturian, Aram (1903–1978)
"Sabre Dance" from *Gayane*. Suite No. 1. Ballet.
Tcherepnin, Alexander (1899–1977)
"Veils and Daggers" from *Georgiana*. Opus 92. Piano and strings.
Weber, Carl Maria von (1786–1826)
*Der Freischütz* (The free shooter). Opera.


WEATHER — see also Clouds, Nature, Rain, Rainbow, Snow, Storm, Water, Wind

Bartók, Béla (1881–1945)
"Melody in the Mist" from *Mikrokosmos*. Book 4. Piano.
Debussy, Claude (1862–1918)
"Brouillards" (Mists) from *Préludes II*. Piano.
Indy, Vincent d' (1851–1931)
"Brouillard" (Fog) from *Poème des montagnes* (Poem of the mountains). Opus 15. Piano.

Ornstein, Leo (1892–
*The Fog.* Orchestral work.
Rieti, Vittorio (1898–
"The Flood" and "The Rainbow" from *L'Arca di Noé* (Noah's Ark).
Orchestral work.
Thomson, Virgil (1896–
"Drought" from *The Plow that Broke the Plains.* Orchestral work.


WEDDING — see also Love, Lovers

Cimarosa, Domenico (1749–1801)
*Il Matrimonio segreto* (The clandestine marriage). Opera.
Glazunov, Alexander (1865–1936)
*Wedding March.* Opus 21. Orchestral work.
Glinka, Mikhail (1804–1857)
"Kamarinskaya" (Wedding song and dance). Orchestral work.
Goldmark, Carl (1830–1915)
*Ländliche Hochzeit* (Rustic wedding symphony). Opus 26.
Orchestral work. Five movements: (1) "Wedding March"
(2) "The Bridal Song" (3) "Serenade" (4) "In the Garden"
(5) "Dance."
Grieg, Edvard (1843–1907)
"Wedding–Day at Troldhaugen" from *Lyric Suite.* Opus 65, No. 6.
Piano.
Kuhnau, Johann (1660–1722)
"Jacob's Wedding" from *Biblical Sonatas.* Harpsichord.
Liszt, Franz (1811–1886)
"Sposalizio" (Wedding) from *Années de pèlerinage: Seconde année:
Italie* (Years of pilgrimage: second year: Italy). Piano.
Mendelssohn, Felix (1809–1847)
"Wedding March" from *A Midsummer Night's Dream.* Opuses 21 and
61a. Orchestral work.
Mozart, Wolfgang Amadeus (1756–1791)
*Le Nozze di Figaro* (The marriage of Figaro). K. 492. Opera.
Prokofiev, Sergei (1891–1953)
"Kije's Wedding" from *Lieutenant Kije.* Opus 60. Orchestral work.
Rimsky–Korsakov, Nikolai (1844–1908)
"Bridal Procession" from *Le Coq d'or* (The golden cockerel).
Orchestral work.
Rossini, Gioacchino (1792–1868)
*La Cambiale di matrimonio* (The marriage contract). Opera.
Saint–Saëns, Camille (1835–1921)
"Wedding–Cake." Opus 76. Strings and piano.
Salzedo, Carlos (1885–1961)
"Wedding Presents." Harp.

Satie, Erik (1866–1925)
   "La Mariée" (The bride) from *Sports et divertissements* (Sports and
      entertainments). Piano.
Schumann, Robert (1810–1856)
   *Die Braut von Messina* (The bride of Messina). Opus 100.
   Orchestral work.
Smetana, Bedrich (1824–1884)
   *The Bartered Bride.* Opera.
Stravinsky, Igor (1882–1971)
   *Les Noces* (The wedding). Ballet with voice.
   "Wedding Dance" from *Four Norwegian Moods.* Orchestral work.
Tchaikovsky, Peter Ilyich (1840–1893)
   "Aurora's Wedding" from *La Belle au bois dormant* (Sleeping beauty).
      Opus 66. Ballet.


WEST INDIES

Benjamin, Arthur (1893–1960)
   *Caribbean Dance.* Orchestral work.
   *Two Jamaican Pieces.* Orchestral work. Two movements:
      (1) "Jamaican Song" (2) "Jamaican Rumba."
Gottschalk, Louis Moreau (1829–1869)
   *Souvenir de Porto Rico* (Recollection of Puerto Rico). Piano.
Prokofiev, Sergei (1891–1953)
   "Dance of the West Indian Slave Girls" from *Romeo and Juliet.*
      Opus 64–ter. Orchestral work.


WILL–o'–the–WISP

Berlioz, Hector (1803–1869)
   "Menuet des feux–follets" (Minuet of the will–o'–the wisps) from
      *La Damnation de Faust* (The damnation of Faust). Opus 24.
      Orchestral work.
Falla, Manuel de (1876–1946)
   "Song of the Will–o'–the–Wisp" from *El Amor brujo* (Love, the
      magician). Ballet.
Liszt, Franz (1811–1886)
   "Feux–Follets" (Will–o'–the–Wisps) from *Etudes d'exécution
      transcendante* (Transcendental Etudes). Piano.
MacDowell, Edward (1860–1908)
   "Will–o'–the–Wisp" from *Woodland Sketches.* Opus 51. Piano.
Rameau, Jean–Philippe (1683–1764)
   "Feux–Follets" (Will–o'–the–Wisps). Harpsichord.

# WIND — see also Storm, Weather

Chopin, Frederic (1810–1849)
Étude in A minor *Winter Wind*. Opus 25, No. 11. Piano.
Couperin, François (1631–1701)
*Les Petits moulins à vent* (The little windmills). Harpsichord.
Ordre 17, No. 2.
Debussy, Claude (1862–1918)
"Ce qu'a vu le vent d'ouest" (What the western wind saw) from
*Préludes I*. Piano.
"Dialogue du vent et de la mer" (Dialogue of the wind and the sea)
from *La Mer* (The sea). Orchestral work.
"Le Vent dans la plaine" (The wind in the plain) from *Préludes I*.
Piano.
"Pour invoquer Pan, Dieu du vent d'été" (To invoke Pan, God of the
summer wind) from *Six Epigraphes antiques* (Six ancient
inscriptions). Piano duet.
Franck, César (1822–1890)
"Psyche Borne Away by the Zephyrs" from *Psyché*. Orchestral
work.
Rameau, Jean–Philippe (1683–1764)
*Les Tourbillons* (The whirlwinds). Harpsichord.


# WINTER — see also Autumn, Seasons, Spring, Summer

Bax, Arnold (1883–1953)
*Winter Legends*. Piano and orchestra.
Bloch, Ernest (1880–1959)
*Hiver–Printemps* (Winter–Spring). Orchestral work.
Chopin, Frederic (1810–1849)
Étude in A minor *Winter Wind*. Opus 25, No. 11. Piano.
Delius, Frederick (1862–1934)
"Winter Landscape" from *North Country Sketches*. Orchestral work.
Glazunov, Alexander (1865–1936)
*The Seasons*. Ballet.
Hadley, Henry (1871–1937)
"Winter" from Symphony No. 2 *The Four Seasons*. Opus 30.
MacDowell, Edward (1860–1908)
"Winter" from *Four Little Poems*. Opus 32. Piano.
Malipiero, Gian Francesco (1882–1973)
"Winter" from Symphony *The Four Seasons*.
Tchaikovsky, Peter Ilyich (1840–1893)
Symphony No. 1 in G minor *Winter Daydreams*. Opus 13.
Vivaldi, Antonio (1678–1741)
"L'Inverno" (Winter) from *Le quattro stagioni* (The four seasons).
Opus 8. Violin and orchestra.

WITCHES — see also Devil

Berlioz, Hector (1803–1869)
"Dream of the Witches' Sabbath" from *Symphonie fantastique* (Fantastic symphony). Opus 14.
Dvořák, Antonín (1841–1904)
*The Noonday Witch*. Opus 108. Orchestral work.
"Witches' Sabbath" from *From the Bohemian Forest*. Opus 68. Piano duet.
Liadov, Anatol (1855–1914)
*Baba Yaga*. Opus 56. Orchestral work.
MacDowell, Edward (1860–1908)
"Witches' Dance" from *Two Fantastic Pieces*. Opus 17. Piano.
Mussorgsky, Modest (1839–1881)
"A Hut on Fowl's Legs" (Baba Yaga) from *Pictures at an Exhibition*. Piano; orchestral work.
Paganini, Niccolò (1782–1840)
*Le Streghe* (Witches' dance). Opus 8. Violin and orchestra.
Smetana, Bedrich (1824–1884)
*Macbeth and the Witches*. Piano.


WOMEN — see also Greek Myths, Historical Figures, Joan of Arc, King Arthur Legends, Royalty, Shakespeare, Witches

Boieldieu, François Adrien (1775–1834)
*La Dame blanche* (The pure woman). Opera.
Debussy, Claude (1862–1918)
"La Fille aux cheveux de lin" (The girl with the flaxen hair) from *Préludes I*. Piano.
Dukas, Paul (1865–1935)
*Ariane et Barbe–bleue* (Ariane and Bluebeard) Opera.
Francaix, Jean (1912–
*Cinq portaits de jeunes filles* (Five portaits of young ladies). Piano.
Five movements: (1) "La Capricieuse" (Capricious)
(2) "La Tendre" (Tender) (3) "La Prétentieuse" (Pretentious)
(4) "La Pensive" (Thoughtful) (5) "La Moderne" (Modern).
Granados, Enrique (1867–1916)
"Quejas o la maja y el ruiseñor" (The maid and the nightingale) from *Goyescas*. Piano.
Khachaturian, Aram (1903–1978)
"Dance of the Rose Maidens" from *Gayane*. Suite No. 1. Ballet.
Prokofiev, Sergei (1891–1953)
"Sailor with Bracelet and Working Women" from *Le Pas d'acier* (The age of steel). Opus 41a. Ballet.
Schumann, Robert (1810–1856)
"Coquette" from *Carnaval*. Opus 9. Piano.

Shostakovich, Dmitri (1906–1975)
*Lady Macbeth of Mzensk.* Opera.
Strauss, Johann Jr. (1825–1899)
*Wein, Weib und Gesang* (Wine, women and song). Opus 333.
Waltz.
Strauss, Richard (1864–1949)
*Die Frau ohne Schatten* (The woman without a shadow). Opus 65.
Opera; orchestral work.
Thomson, Virgil (1896–
*The Mother of us All.* Opera.
Tommasini, Vincenzo (1878–1950)
*La Donne di buon umore* (The good–humored ladies). Ballet.
Turina, Joaquín (1882–1949)
*Mujeres españolas* (Spanish women). Opus 17. Piano.
Three movements: (1) "La Madrilena classica" (The classic woman
of Madrid) (2) "La Anduluza sentimental" (The sentimental woman
of Andalusía) (3) "La Corena coqueta" (The coquette of Corena).
"Siluetas de la calzada" (Portrait of a woman in shoes) from *Sanlúcar
de Barrameda.* Opus 24. Piano.
Wolf, Hugo (1860–1903)
*Penthesilea.* Orchestral work. Three movements: (1) "The Departure
of Amazons for Troy" (2) "Penthesilea's Dream of the Feast of the
Roses" (3) "Combats, Passions, Frenzy, Annihilation."
Wolf–Ferrari, Ermanno (1876–1948)
*Il Segreto di Susanna* (The secret of Suzanne). Opera.

# BIBLIOGRAPHY

## BOOKS

Arnold, Denis. *The New Oxford Companion to Music.*
Oxford, Oxford University Press, 1984.

Cross, Milton. *The New Complete Stories of the Great Operas.*
Garden City, NY, Doubleday and Company Inc., 1955.
*The New Complete More Stories of the Great Operas.*
Garden City, NY, Doubleday and Company Inc., 1980.

Ewen, David. *The Complete Book of 20th Century Music.*
Englewood Cliffs, NJ, Prentice–Hall Inc., 1959.
*Music for the Millions.* New York, Arco Publishing
Company, 1944.

Gillespie, John. *Five Centuries of Keyboard Music.* New York,
Dover Publications Inc., 1965.

Hutcheson, Ernest. *The Literature of the Piano.* New York,
Alfred Knopf, 1964.

Upton, George P. and Borowski, Felix. *The Standard Concert Guide.*
Garden City, NY, Blue Ribbon Books, 1940.

## DICTIONARIES

Apel, Willi. *Harvard Dictionary of Music.* Cambridge, MA, Belknap
Press of Harvard University Press, 1972.

Sadie, Stanley, editor. *The New Grove Dictionary of Music and
Musicians.* London, Macmillan Publishers Ltd., 1980.

Slonimsky, Nicolas. *Baker's Biographical Dictionary of Music.*
New York, Schirmer Books, 1984.

Vinton, John, editor. *Dictionary of Contemporary Music.* New York,
E.P. Dutton and Company Inc., 1974.

# ENCYCLOPEDIAS

Bohle, Bruce, editor. *The International Cyclopedia of Music and Musicians.* New York, Dodd, Mead and Company, 1975.

Cross, Milton and Ewen, David. *(The Milton Cross) New Encyclopedia of the Great Composers and their Music.* Garden City, NY., Doubleday and Company Inc., 1969.

Ewen, David. *Encyclopedia of Concert Music.* New York, Hill and Wang, 1959.

Westrup, J.A. and Harrison, F. Ll. *The New Encyclopedia of Music.* New York, W.W. Norton and Company Inc., 1976.

# CATALOGUES

Musical Heritage Society. *1987 Master Catalog.* Ocean, NJ, Musical Heritage Society, 1987.

Tynan, William, editor. *Schwann Catalog.* New York, Schwann Publications, 1987.

Walker, Malcolm, editor. *Gramophone Classical Catalogue.* Harrow, Middlesex, General Gramophone Publishers Ltd., 1987.

# INDEX OF SUBJECT HEADINGS